Distinguished Wisdom Presents...
"Living Proverbs"—Vol. 2

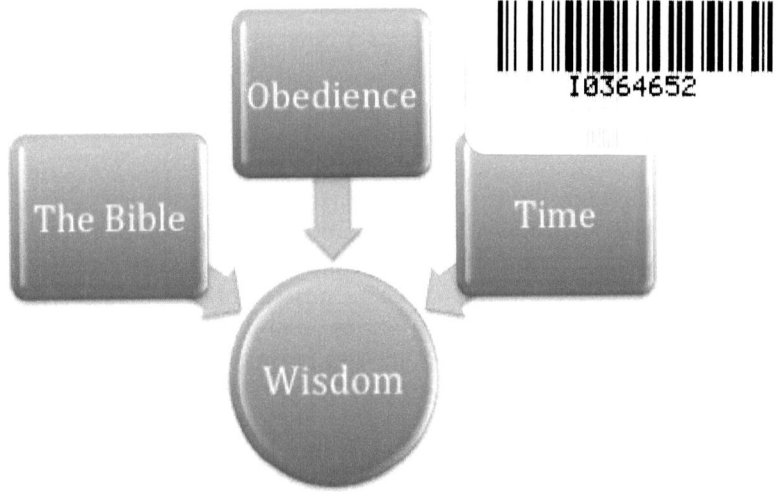

— *Over 500 Wisdom Nuggets
To Enrich Your Life* —

Pastor Terrance Levise Turner, MBA

Well Spoken Inc. | Nashville, TN

© 2018 Terrance Levise Turner

All rights reserved. No part of this publication may be reproduced, scanned, transmitted or distributed in any printed or electronic or mechanical forms or methods, including photocopying, recording, or other without prior written permission of the publisher, except in the case of brief select quotations embodied in critical reviews and certain other noncommercial uses permitted by copyright law. For permission requests, write to the publisher, addressed below.

Unless otherwise indicated, all Scripture quotations are taken from the King James Version of the Bible. Unless otherwise indicated all original quotes are those of
Pastor Terrance Levise Turner.

Well Spoken Inc.
P.O. Box 291806 Nashville, TN. 37229
WellSpokenInc@bellsouth.net
www.TerranceTurnerBooks.com

Ordering Information

Quantity sales. Special discounts are available on quantity purchases by corporations, associations, and others. For details, contact the "Special Sales Department" at the address above.

Cover design by Ryan Urz/Susan of LSDdesign/99Designs.com
Book design by Terrance L. Turner

Printed in the United States of America

ISBN	9781732763906	and	9781732763937	paperback
ISBN	9781732763913	and	9781732763944	hardcover
ISBN	9781732763920	and	9781732763951	Ebook

This book is dedicated to young people of today and of future generations. I desire that they have a solid understanding of God and His principles for life and thereby have a successful, prosperous, safe, and godly life.

Contents

Acknowledgements VII
Introduction X
"Living Proverbs"–Vol.2 1
Final Word 253
About The Author 255

VI

Acknowledgements

I would like to acknowledge the love and support of my wife, Dr. Avis Turner. She is my partner in life, and the gift that God has given me to help accomplish His purposes in life. Her support and encouragement has helped to enable me to reach the potential God has invested in me. She is a *true* wife. We are better together, and together God is enabling us to reach the world.

Again, I would like to give everlasting thanks to my mother, Geraldine Key, for the foundation of truth and example she laid for my brothers and I. She is the reason I know God as my Heavenly Father and the Lord Jesus Christ as my Savior. She continues to be a support and encouragement as I strive to fulfill God's purposes for my life.

I acknowledge the solid example of faith, faithfulness, and morality that I gained from my grandmother, Wilma Starks, and grandfather, Clarence Young. They both were sources of stability in my life. Their examples will continue to live on in all that I do.

Thank you to those who encouraged the writing of volume 1, as I shared "wisdom nuggets" on social media. Several individuals, in the early stages, encouraged me to keep sharing. Their words of support contributed to the hastening of the development of volume 2. I would like to acknowledge especially Mrs. Morgan and Mr. William Freeman.

I thank God for all the teachers and preachers of wisdom and instruction over my lifetime. Thank God for Rev. Brockway, Bishop Phillip Gardner, missionary Mary Archie, Pastor Charles Cowan, Bishop TD Jakes, Joyce Meyer, Dr. Mike Murdock, and many others that has inspired my life. Thank God for inspirational and motivational teachers such as Les Brown, Brian Tracy, Dr. John Maxwell; as well as great leaders in our society such as Gen. Colin Powell. Also, I recognize the impact of great educational leaders upon my life, such as the late Dr. James A. Hefner, former president of Tennessee State University. My life has been impacted by great leaders in wisdom, instruction, and by example. My mother laid the foundation, and Jehovah God my Heavenly Father has built upon that foundation the right keystones, starting with my wife, Dr. Avis Turner, for a successful life.

Introduction

The Purpose of "Living Proverbs".

The purpose of "Living Proverbs" is derived from the purpose of my company Well Spoken, Incorporated in Nashville, Tennessee. In 2005, God inspired me to start a company with the purpose of communicating the spoken word in a clear, distinct manner that easily conveyed understanding to the listener. Our primary product has been audio books. Thus far, we have focused on biblical material. However, because of my expanded education in business and leadership, we will also add other products to our offerings. Well Spoken Inc. is also the company through which I accept professional speaking engagements. My wife, Dr. Turner, and I founded and operate the company together.

    The foundational Scripture that God gave me that inspired the company is Nehemiah 8:7–8. It says,

> Also Jeshua, and Bani, and Sherebiah, Jamin, Akkub, Shabbethai, Hodijah, Maaseiah, Kelita, Azariah, Jozabad, Hanan, Pelaiah, and the Levites, caused the people to understand the law: and the people stood in their place.
> So they read in the book in the law of God distinctly, and gave the sense, and caused them to understand the reading.

– Nehemiah 8:7–8

This particular Scripture indicates that the Levites helped the people to understand the law of God, and the people became secure in their place in the land. They became stable as a result of gaining understanding. The Levites read in the book of the law of God "distinctly", and gave the "sense" or meaning or policy or prosperity of the Scripture, and they helped the people to understand what was read. The Levites carried out a specific and important, vital function to the people becoming prosperous through understanding the Word of God that was spoken by the priests.

    The Scripture says, "So they read in the book of the law of God distinctly..." This is where God gave me the name for our brand *"Distinguished Wisdom Presents..."* the Levites helped the people to *"distinguish"* what the Word of God was saying or what it really meant. One meaning of the word "distinguish" in the Webster's dictionary is *"to recognize plainly by any of the senses"*. The root meaning is *"to prick or pierce apart"*. The word "distinct" is defined as *"clearly marked off; plain; well defined; unmistakable."* God used the Levites to clearly define His Word for the people so that it would be unmistakable what He meant. God wanted them to understand His true purposes for giving His laws, which is for our good.

    When God gave me this brand and assignment for *"Distinguished Wisdom Presents..."* He indicated to me that he had anointed me to share wisdom in a *distinct* manner. Through my study of the book of Proverbs from childhood, I developed a love for wisdom and the Word of God. My

education in communications helped prepare me to speak God's Word. God gave me the name of the company Well Spoken, Incorporated as a way of ministering His Word in a specialized manner to those who needed to understand.

I began to share *"Living Proverbs"* as wisdom nuggets to friends and followers on social media as a means of sharing God's Word to encourage, inspire, and inform. The platform of social media has allowed an expanded reach of God's Word into the world for both believers as well as secular society. God has a need for those willing to share his Word with the world. 2 Chronicles 15:3 indicate to us God's need for a *willing vessel* to share His Word. This is what it says,

> Now for a long season Israel hath been without the true God, and without a teaching priest, and without law.
>
> −2 Chronicles 15:3

God needs "teaching priests" who will teach His Word and bring understanding of His laws to society. This is my purpose, to fulfill God's commission of spreading His Word and ways to the hearts of His people. This book is straightforward just like volume 1. It goes directly into each of the "Living Proverbs". They are numbered in order to differentiate one from the other and also to be able to reference each one individually. They are appropriately supported by rightly applied scripture, which further the readers understanding. The goal of the book is not to develop a new doctrine; rather, it is to *reveal* the wisdom of God that is contained in the written doctrine of Scripture.

Pastor Terrance Levise Turner

3 John 2 says, "Beloved, I wish above all things thou mayest prosper and be in health, even as thy soul prospereth." This is my prayer and desire for you as you read and meditate this book *Distinguished Wisdom Presents…"Living Proverbs"– Volume 2*. *"May your life be enriched by the words of wisdom!"*

–Pastor Terrance Levise Turner

"Living Proverbs"–Vol.2

531. Resist being offended, rather, be *effective*.

The discretion of a man deferreth his anger; and it is his glory to pass over a transgression.

–Proverbs 19:11

532. In an adversarial environment, do not allow *petty strife* to sabotage the mission or threaten the team.

And there was a strife between the herdmen of Abram's cattle and the herdmen of Lot's cattle: and the Canaanite and the Perizzite dwelled then in the land. And Abram said unto Lot, Let there be no strife, I pray thee, between me and thee, and between my herdmen and thy herdmen; for we be brethren

Is not the whole land before thee? separate thyself, I pray thee, from me: if thou wilt take the left hand, then I will go to the right; or if thou depart to the right hand, then I will go to the left.

– Genesis 13:7–9

533. A great idea, plus diligent effort are the keys to *independent wealth*. Success is available to the *diligent*.

He becometh poor that dealeth with a slack hand: but the hand of the diligent maketh rich.

–Proverbs 10:4

534. There is a spirit of restriction, limitation, fear, and terror that seeks to hinder courageous progress. Yet, we can overcome it through faith. The just shall live by faith!

Be strong and courageous, be not afraid nor dismayed for the king of Assyria, nor for all the multitude that is with him: for there be more with us than with him: with him is an arm of flesh; but with us is the Lord our God to help us, and to fight our battles. And the people rested themselves upon the words of Hezekiah king of Judah.

–2 Chronicles 32:7–8

535. Take time to *"till"* and cultivate your mind. Pull up *weeds* of doubt, fear, and negativity. Avoid fruitless people,

endeavors, and behaviors. Plant *seeds* of faith and possibility; and reap a harvest of abundant provision!

He that tilleth his land shall be satisfied with bread: but he that followeth vain persons is void of understanding.

— Proverbs 12:11

536. Spend time in the Bible long enough to become fully *acquainted* with the "*author and finisher*" of your faith.

Acquaint now thyself with him, and be at peace: thereby good shall come unto thee.

— Job 22:21

537. Here is the priority of creativity: 1) *birth* what you are pregnant with 2) *tend* to what's already birthed 3) *harvest* what's already grown.

The slothful man roasteth not that which he took in hunting: but the substance of a diligent man is precious.

— Proverbs 12:27

538. In regards to large dreams, we walk by faith and not by sight, and *soon* we will see.

For we walk by faith, not by sight.

—2 Corinthians 5:7

Now faith is the substance of things hoped for, the evidence of things not seen.

– Hebrews 11:1

539. Every life has challenges, however, what determines whether we fall, or we stand, will be the *foundation* we build upon.

Therefore whosoever heareth these sayings of mine, and doeth them, I will liken him unto a wise man, which built his house upon a rock: And the rain descended, and the floods came, and the winds blew, and beat upon that house; and it fell not: for it was founded upon a rock. And every one that heareth these sayings of mine, and doeth them not, shall be likened unto a foolish man, which built his house upon the sand: And the rain descended, and the floods came, and the winds blew, and beat upon that house; and it fell: and great was the fall of it.

– Matthew 7:24–27

540. I'd rather *step out* and find out, than *sit back* and continue to *lack*.

And there were four leprous men at the entering in of the gate: and they said one to another, Why sit we here until we die? If we say, We will enter into the city, then the famine is in the city, and we shall die there: and if we sit still here, we die also. Now therefore come, and let us fall unto the host of

the Syrians: if they save us alive, we shall live; and if they kill us, we shall but die.

–2 Kings 7:3–4

541. If God has given you something that can benefit society, don't fail to *launch*, due to fear of failure or lack of perfection. Launch by faith and *update* as you go: just like every innovation or new technology.

For we walk by faith, not by sight.

–2 Corinthians 5:7

Now faith is the substance of things hoped for, the evidence of things not seen.

– Hebrews 11:1

542. You never have to be in competition with anyone else as long as you are doing *your* thing. You're only in competition with others when you're doing *their* thing.

But let every man prove his own work, and then shall he have rejoicing in himself alone, and not in another.

– Galatians 6:4

543. The eternal hope of eternal life is found in the Eternal God, The Lord Jesus Christ.

For I know that my redeemer liveth, and that he shall stand at the latter day upon the earth: And though after my skin worms destroy this body, yet in my flesh shall I see God: Whom I shall see for myself, and mine eyes shall behold, and not another; though my reins be consumed within me.

– Job 19:25–27

544. The best way to predict and influence the future is to *create it*.

A man's belly shall be satisfied with the fruit of his mouth; and with the increase of his lips shall he be filled. Death and life are in the power of the tongue: and they that love it shall eat the fruit thereof.

– Proverbs 18:20–21

545. Intelligence isn't about knowing everything. Intelligence is *recognizing* you don't: yet having the willingness and ability to *learn*.

Also, that the soul be without knowledge, it is not good; and he that hasteth with his feet sinneth.

– Proverbs 19:2

546. A lifetime of righteous living establishes you for a lifetime of riches and security. You shall not be *moved!*

A man shall not be established by wickedness: but the root of the righteous shall not be moved.

– Proverbs 12:3

547. We must study the Bible in order to establish our souls in truth. We must study *functional* knowledge and facts to be current in its *usability*.

Wisdom is the principal thing; therefore get wisdom: and with all thy getting get understanding.

– Proverbs 4:7

548. Success breeds *confidence*. Confidence breeds *success*.

Who is as the wise man? and who knoweth the interpretation of a thing? a man's wisdom maketh his face to shine, and the boldness of his face shall be changed.

– Ecclesiastes 8:1

549. *Circumcise* the flesh from overeating, oversleeping, overspending, and overindulgence: it's the key to success and *overcoming!*

What advantage then hath the Jew? or what profit is there of circumcision? Much every way: chiefly, because that unto them were committed the oracles of God. For what if some did not believe? shall their unbelief make the faith of God without effect? God forbid: yea, let God be true, but every man a liar; as it is written, That thou mightest be justified in thy sayings, and mightest overcome when thou art judged.

– Romans 3:1–4

550. I would rather be *God–handled* than manhandled. Manhandling leads to abuse. God handling leads to perfect use.

Humble yourselves therefore under the mighty hand of God, that he may exalt you in due time: Casting all your care upon him; for he careth for you.

–1 Peter 5:6–7

551. Consensus does not define *correctness*. Consensus does not negate consequences. Only the unyielding laws of God's truth will decide eventual outcomes.

Every one that is proud in heart is an abomination to the Lord: though hand join in hand, he shall not be unpunished.

– Proverbs 16:5

552. May God give us all an *abundance* mentality that accepts the abundant provision he has made available to us all from the beginning.

And the Lord God formed man of the dust of the ground, and breathed into his nostrils the breath of life; and man became a living soul. And the Lord God planted a garden eastward in Eden; and there he put the man whom he had formed. And out of the ground made the Lord God to grow every tree that is pleasant to the sight, and good for food; the tree of life also

in the midst of the garden, and the tree of knowledge of good and evil. And a river went out of Eden to water the garden; and from thence it was parted, and became into four heads. The name of the first is Pison: that is it which compasseth the whole land of Havilah, where there is gold; And the gold of that land is good: there is bdellium and the onyx stone. And the name of the second river is Gihon: the same is it that compasseth the whole land of Ethiopia. And the name of the third river is Hiddekel: that is it which goeth toward the east of Assyria. And the fourth river is Euphrates. And the Lord God took the man, and put him into the garden of Eden to dress it and to keep it. And the Lord God commanded the man, saying, Of every tree of the garden thou mayest freely eat.

— Genesis 2:7–16

553. Significant change goes *against the grain*.

And when they found them not, they drew Jason and certain brethren unto the rulers of the city, crying, These that have turned the world upside down are come hither also.

— Acts 17:6

554. No matter what may be your opposition at this moment, God is greater. He will help you triumph. God specializes in winning battles where the odds are stacked against his children. Be not afraid. You will *triumph!*

When thou goest out to battle against thine enemies, and seest horses, and chariots, and a people more than thou, be not afraid of them: for the Lord thy God is with thee, which brought thee up out of the land of Egypt. And it shall be, when ye are come nigh unto the battle, that the priest shall approach and speak unto the people, And shall say unto them, Hear, O Israel, ye approach this day unto battle against your enemies: let not your hearts faint, fear not, and do not tremble, neither be ye terrified because of them; For the Lord your God is he that goeth with you, to fight for you against your enemies, to save you.

– Deuteronomy 20:1–4

555. Wherever you are in life and whatever you are facing, God can reach you. God can save you. God does hear you. God does love you. He's helping you now, this very moment! In Jesus name. Amen!

Behold, the Lord's hand is not shortened, that it cannot save; neither his ear heavy, that it cannot hear.

– Isaiah 59:1

556. Nobody can keep you from getting your money, but you! You're not in competition with anybody, but you. You're in *cooperation* with God.

Know ye not that they which run in a race run all, but one receiveth the prize? So run, that ye may obtain. And every man that striveth for the mastery is temperate in all things.

Now they do it to obtain a corruptible crown; but we an incorruptible. I therefore so run, not as uncertainly; so fight I, not as one that beateth the air: But I keep under my body, and bring it into subjection: lest that by any means, when I have preached to others, I myself should be a castaway.

−1 Corinthians 9:24–27

557. You never can lose in *giving*.

There is that scattereth, and yet increaseth; and there is that withholdeth more than is meet, but it tendeth to poverty. The liberal soul shall be made fat: and he that watereth shall be watered also himself.

− Proverbs 11:24–25

558. No matter how you feel, *keep it real*. Real is, you're strong! Real is, you're powerful! Real is, you're successful! Real is, you're a winner! Real is, you've overcome! No matter how you feel, *keep it real!*

Rejoice in the Lord always: and again I say, Rejoice. Let your moderation be known unto all men. The Lord is at hand. Be careful for nothing; but in every thing by prayer and supplication with thanksgiving let your requests be made known unto God. And the peace of God, which passeth all understanding, shall keep your hearts and minds through Christ Jesus. Finally, brethren, whatsoever things are true, whatsoever things are honest, whatsoever things are just, whatsoever things are pure, whatsoever things are lovely,

whatsoever things are of good report; if there be any virtue, and if there be any praise, think on these things. Those things, which ye have both learned, and received, and heard, and seen in me, do: and the God of peace shall be with you.

– Philippians 4:4–9

559. A woman of *virtue* is a woman of great worth. She is a woman of great value. She increases the value of her husband and family. She is a great resource in society.

Who can find a virtuous woman? for her price is far above rubies. The heart of her husband doth safely trust in her, so that he shall have no need of spoil. She will do him good and not evil all the days of her life. She seeketh wool, and flax, and worketh willingly with her hands. She is like the merchants' ships; she bringeth her food from afar. She riseth also while it is yet night, and giveth meat to her household, and a portion to her maidens. She considereth a field, and buyeth it: with the fruit of her hands she planteth a vineyard. She girdeth her loins with strength, and strengtheneth her arms. She perceiveth that her merchandise is good: her candle goeth not out by night. She layeth her hands to the spindle, and her hands hold the distaff. She stretcheth out her hand to the poor; yea, she reacheth forth her hands to the needy. She is not afraid of the snow for her household: for all her household are clothed with scarlet. She maketh herself coverings of tapestry; her clothing is silk and purple. Her husband is known in the gates, when he sitteth among the elders of the land. She maketh fine linen, and selleth it; and delivereth girdles unto the merchant. Strength and honour are her

clothing; and she shall rejoice in time to come. She openeth her mouth with wisdom; and in her tongue is the law of kindness. She looketh well to the ways of her household, and eateth not the bread of idleness. Her children arise up, and call her blessed; her husband also, and he praiseth her. Many daughters have done virtuously, but thou excellest them all. Favour is deceitful, and beauty is vain: but a woman that feareth the Lord, she shall be praised. Give her of the fruit of her hands; and let her own works praise her in the gates.

– Proverbs 31:10–31

560. A great seed never goes without an abundant harvest. It's always good to sow greatly to bless others. Yet expect, desire, and anticipate your harvest from God. He always *pays big!*

But this I say, He which soweth sparingly shall reap also sparingly; and he which soweth bountifully shall reap also bountifully. Every man according as he purposeth in his heart, so let him give; not grudgingly, or of necessity: for God loveth a cheerful giver. And God is able to make all grace abound toward you; that ye, always having all sufficiency in all things, may abound to every good work.

−2 Corinthians 9:6–8

561. Without God in your life there is no *true* light. There is only guessing, wishing, and hoping. Jesus is the Light of the world, give Him your heart and hand, He will guide you through life.

There was a man sent from God, whose name was John. The same came for a witness, to bear witness of the Light, that all men through him might believe. He was not that Light, but was sent to bear witness of that Light. That was the true Light, which lighteth every man that cometh into the world. He was in the world, and the world was made by him, and the world knew him not. He came unto his own, and his own received him not. But as many as received him, to them gave he power to become the sons of God, even to them that believe on his name.

– John 1:6–12

562. Everyday we have *two* choices. We can wake up singing or we can wake up complaining. We always have a choice.

It is a good thing to give thanks unto the Lord, and to sing praises unto thy name, O most High: to shew forth thy lovingkindness in the morning, and thy faithfulness every night.

– Psalm 92:1–2

563. Seeking the LORD, and doing His principles, shall pay off. You lay up an inheritance against the times of evil in the earth. You will be sustained in the times of famine.

The Lord knoweth the days of the upright: and their inheritance shall be for ever. They shall not be ashamed in the evil time: and in the days of famine they shall be satisfied. But

the wicked shall perish, and the enemies of the Lord shall be as the fat of lambs: they shall consume; into smoke shall they consume away.

– Psalm 37:18–20

564. God has certain laws and principles that transcend all rights, order, position, or even favor. The *law of diligence* will work for whosoever will work it. The spoils go to the hand of the diligent!

The hand of the diligent shall bear rule: but the slothful shall be under tribute.

– Proverbs 12:24

565. Stop complaining and *get busy!*

The hand of the diligent shall bear rule: but the slothful shall be under tribute.

– Proverbs 12:24

566. May we seek to please the LORD in our behavior today as we interact with one another. Let us walk justly and compassionately toward others. And let the light of God's love shine through us today.

Thus speaketh the Lord of hosts, saying, Execute true judgment, and shew mercy and compassions every man to his brother: and oppress not the widow, nor the fatherless, the

stranger, nor the poor; and let none of you imagine evil against his brother in your heart.

— Zechariah 7:9–10

567. You can't argue against *results*.

For we dare not make ourselves of the number, or compare ourselves with some that commend themselves: but they measuring themselves by themselves, and comparing themselves among themselves, are not wise.

—2 Corinthians 10:12

568. Give help without a lot of *hype!*

Or he that exhorteth, on exhortation: he that giveth, let him do it with simplicity; he that ruleth, with diligence; he that sheweth mercy, with cheerfulness.

— Romans 12:8

569. Solve problems *quickly* before excess damage occurs.

The beginning of strife is as when one letteth out water: therefore leave off contention, before it be meddled with.

— Proverbs 17:14

570. Jesus was made unto you wisdom for this day. Place a demand on Him as your source by calling on His name during the day. He will help you with every challenge of life.

But of him are ye in Christ Jesus, who of God is made unto us wisdom, and righteousness, and sanctification, and redemption.

–1 Corinthians 1:30

Get wisdom, get understanding: forget it not; neither decline from the words of my mouth. Forsake her not, and she shall preserve thee: love her, and she shall keep thee. Wisdom is the principal thing; therefore get wisdom: and with all thy getting get understanding. Exalt her, and she shall promote thee: she shall bring thee to honour, when thou dost embrace her.

– Proverbs 4:5–8

571. God has already seen and solved the problems and issues that are just now arriving to your life. He's not nervous. You shouldn't be either. He only wants you to *participate* with Him in the victory through prayer and faith.

Rejoice in the Lord always: and again I say, Rejoice. Let your moderation be known unto all men. The Lord is at hand. Be careful for nothing; but in every thing by prayer and supplication with thanksgiving let your requests be made known unto God. And the peace of God, which passeth all understanding, shall keep your hearts and minds through Christ Jesus. Finally, brethren, whatsoever things are true, whatsoever things are honest, whatsoever things are just, whatsoever things are pure, whatsoever things are lovely, whatsoever things are of good report; if there be any virtue,

and if there be any praise, think on these things. Those things, which ye have both learned, and received, and heard, and seen in me, do: and the God of peace shall be with you.

– Philippians 4:4–9

572. As people get to know you, may they know, trust, and rely upon your *word* more than your name or reputation. Reputation can be misconstrued, but your word is either true or false.

I will worship toward thy holy temple, and praise thy name for thy lovingkindness and for thy truth: for thou hast magnified thy word above all thy name.

– Psalm 138:2

573. Sometimes there are extended seasons of warfare. And, you must be as diligent as the Devil is opposing you in your spiritual warfare against him.

For though we walk in the flesh, we do not war after the flesh: (For the weapons of our warfare are not carnal, but mighty through God to the pulling down of strong holds;) Casting down imaginations, and every high thing that exalteth itself against the knowledge of God, and bringing into captivity every thought to the obedience of Christ.

–2 Corinthians 10:3–5

574. The purpose of obeying God's principles is to receive the promised benefits, which He desires for you. He desires to bless you. Please participate with Him, by obeying his principles.

Humble yourselves therefore under the mighty hand of God, that he may exalt you in due time.

–1 Peter 5:6

575. Don't settle for your circumstances. Rather, keep striving for what's in your DNA. Success is in your DNA! Winning is in your DNA! Prosperity is in your DNA! You were born to win! And made to succeed!

And God said, Let us make man in our image, after our likeness: and let them have dominion over the fish of the sea, and over the fowl of the air, and over the cattle, and over all the earth, and over every creeping thing that creepeth upon the earth. So God created man in his own image, in the image of God created he him; male and female created he them. And God blessed them, and God said unto them, Be fruitful, and multiply, and replenish the earth, and subdue it: and have dominion over the fish of the sea, and over the fowl of the air, and over every living thing that moveth upon the earth.

– Genesis 1:26–28

576. You have something special to give to society and life. God has *invested* a portion of Himself into you. He has given you the privilege of *creatively* giving it away.

As every man hath received the gift, even so minister the same one to another, as good stewards of the manifold grace of God.

−1 Peter 4:10

577. Everything takes time; but when it happens, it's *right on time!*

He hath made every thing beautiful in his time: also he hath set the world in their heart, so that no man can find out the work that God maketh from the beginning to the end.

– Ecclesiastes 3:11

578. Live everyday to the *full.* Enjoy your life to the full today. Be thankful for our daily bread. Be thankful for our jobs, families, health, and home. Believe God for long–life, full of plenty. Nevertheless, be thankful for today's *manna!*

And when the dew that lay was gone up, behold, upon the face of the wilderness there lay a small round thing, as small as the hoar frost on the ground. And when the children of Israel saw it, they said one to another, It is manna: for they wist not what it was. And Moses said unto them, This is the bread which the Lord hath given you to eat.

– Exodus 16:14–15

579. Choose to love all people, everywhere, *all the time.*

A new commandment I give unto you, That ye love one another; as I have loved you, that ye also love one another.

– John 13:34

580. As long as we continue to stretch forward; *better* is always ahead.

For to him that is joined to all the living there is hope: for a living dog is better than a dead lion. For the living know that they shall die: but the dead know not any thing, neither have they any more a reward; for the memory of them is forgotten. Also their love, and their hatred, and their envy, is now perished; neither have they any more a portion for ever in any thing that is done under the sun. Go thy way, eat thy bread with joy; and drink thy wine with a merry heart; for God now accepteth thy works. Let thy garments be always white; and let thy head lack no ointment. Live joyfully with the wife whom thou lovest all the days of the life of thy vanity, which he hath given thee under the sun, all the days of thy vanity: for that is thy portion in this life, and in thy labour which thou takest under the sun. Whatsoever thy hand findeth to do, do it with thy might; for there is no work, nor device, nor knowledge, nor wisdom, in the grave, whither thou goest. I returned, and saw under the sun, that the race is not to the swift, nor the battle to the strong, neither yet bread to the wise, nor yet riches to men of understanding, nor yet favour to men of skill; but time and chance happeneth to them all.

– Ecclesiastes 9:4–11

581. May we submit ourselves unto God, so that his agenda and kingdom will prevail, and not our own. In doing so, we will prosper. He wishes above all things that we prosper, be in health, even as our souls prosper.

Humble yourselves therefore under the mighty hand of God, that he may exalt you in due time.

–1 Peter 5:6

582. In regards to wisdom, wealth, and family: You have come to your family and to the earth for such a time as this. You are the Joseph, Queen Esther, King Solomon, and Queen of Sheba for your family and *generation!*

And Joseph said unto them, Fear not: for am I in the place of God? But as for you, ye thought evil against me; but God meant it unto good, to bring to pass, as it is this day, to save much people alive. Now therefore fear ye not: I will nourish you, and your little ones. And he comforted them, and spake kindly unto them.

– Genesis 50:19–21

And when the queen of Sheba heard of the fame of Solomon concerning the name of the Lord, she came to prove him with hard questions. And she came to Jerusalem with a very great train, with camels that bare spices, and very much gold, and precious stones: and when she was come to Solomon, she communed with him of all that was in her heart. And Solomon

told her all her questions: there was not any thing hid from the king, which he told her not.

−1 Kings 10:1–3

So king Solomon exceeded all the kings of the earth for riches and for wisdom. And all the earth sought to Solomon, to hear his wisdom, which God had put in his heart.

−1 Kings 10:23–24

For if thou altogether holdest thy peace at this time, then shall there enlargement and deliverance arise to the Jews from another place; but thou and thy father's house shall be destroyed: and who knoweth whether thou art come to the kingdom for such a time as this?

− Esther 4:14

583. May the favor of the LORD rest upon your work today. May you prosper and have peace. May wisdom and exceptional performance be manifested in your efforts, and may you be abundantly compensated with rich rewards. In Jesus name. Amen.

And let the beauty of the Lord our God be upon us: and establish thou the work of our hands upon us; yea, the work of our hands establish thou it.

− Psalm 90:17

584. The courage to actually engage in positive action increases the likelihood of multiplying successful outcomes.

Now therefore perform the doing of it; that as there was a readiness to will, so there may be a performance also out of that which ye have. For if there be first a willing mind, it is accepted according to that a man hath, and not according to that he hath not.

–2 Corinthians 8:11–12

585. Money without a specific assignment is *wasted*.

Wilt thou set thine eyes upon that which is not? for riches certainly make themselves wings; they fly away as an eagle toward heaven.

– Proverbs 23:5

586. You must take steps of faith and actively be pursuing something *tangible* for God to give you favor on; in order to see the mighty hand of God's "*super*" on your *natural*. You must be taking steps for Him to order!

The steps of a good man are ordered by the Lord: and he delighteth in his way.

– Psalm 37:23

587. Lord, without You, I can do nothing. With You, I can do all things through Christ, which strengthens me!

I can do all things through Christ, which strengtheneth me.

– Philippians 4:13

588. Everyday we are *running against the clock* in order to maximize the life we have left. We must exercise, eat right, and maximize every opportunity, in order to maximize the value we can bring to our families, life, and ourselves.

So teach us to number our days, that we may apply our hearts unto wisdom.

– Psalm 90:12

589. God has a plan. We must be committed to His plan and submitted to His plan, in order to see the lifetime rewards manifest in our life.

Humble yourselves therefore under the mighty hand of God, that he may exalt you in due time.

–1 Peter 5:6

590. Submit yourself long enough in prayer and Bible study before God in order for Him to give you clear direction for every major decision.

The meek will he guide in judgment: and the meek will he teach his way.

– Psalm 25:9

591. Most people hear wisdom: few actually *obey* it. However, those who do, receive the reward.

Therefore whosoever heareth these sayings of mine, and doeth them, I will liken him unto a wise man, which built his house upon a rock: And the rain descended, and the floods came, and the winds blew, and beat upon that house; and it fell not: for it was founded upon a rock. And every one that heareth these sayings of mine, and doeth them not, shall be likened unto a foolish man, which built his house upon the sand: And the rain descended, and the floods came, and the winds blew, and beat upon that house; and it fell: and great was the fall of it.

– Matthew 7:24–27

592. You will overcome your opposition in spite of what may be going on in the world. Trust in God. Keep your faith. Be bold as a *lion!* You will come out victorious overall through trusting and obeying God. In Jesus name. Amen!

It is good that thou shouldest take hold of this; yea, also from this withdraw not thine hand: for he that feareth God shall come forth of them all.

– Ecclesiastes 7:18

593. Worrying never helps anything. Prayer helps *everything.*

Rejoice in the Lord always: and again I say, Rejoice. Let your moderation be known unto all men. The Lord is at hand. Be careful for nothing; but in every thing by prayer and supplication with thanksgiving let your requests be made known unto God. And the peace of God, which passeth all understanding, shall keep your hearts and minds through Christ Jesus. Finally, brethren, whatsoever things are true, whatsoever things are honest, whatsoever things are just, whatsoever things are pure, whatsoever things are lovely, whatsoever things are of good report; if there be any virtue, and if there be any praise, think on these things. Those things, which ye have both learned, and received, and heard, and seen in me, do: and the God of peace shall be with you.

– Philippians 4:4–9

594. Only money with an *assignment* has a future.

Wilt thou set thine eyes upon that which is not? For riches certainly make themselves wings; they fly away as an eagle toward heaven.

– Proverbs 23:5

595. God has a specific plan and destiny for your life, and it's *good!* Jesus Christ is the "author and finisher" of our faith. He has preordained our path and success. We are His workmanship, made in His image and likeness. We were made for success and destined for greatness!

For we are his workmanship, created in Christ Jesus unto good works, which God hath before ordained that we should walk in them.

– Ephesians 2:10

596. A believer that fails to pray will *fail*.

And he spake a parable unto them *to this end*, that men ought always to pray, and not to faint.

– Luke 18:1

597. There are some practices that should be followed religiously: like a consistent, systematic practice of prayer, fasting, bible study, and worship of God. They are the keys to a strong, stable, reliable life.

And he spake a parable unto them *to this end*, that men ought always to pray, and not to faint.

– Luke 18:1

It is a good thing to give thanks unto the Lord, and to sing praises unto thy name, O most High: to shew forth thy lovingkindness in the morning, and thy faithfulness every night.

– Psalm 92:1–2

And Jesus said unto them, Because of your unbelief: for verily I say unto you, If ye have faith as a grain of mustard seed, ye

shall say unto this mountain, Remove hence to yonder place; and it shall remove; and nothing shall be impossible unto you. Howbeit this kind goeth not out but by prayer and fasting.

– Matthew 17:20–21

Therefore whosoever heareth these sayings of mine, and doeth them, I will liken him unto a wise man, which built his house upon a rock: And the rain descended, and the floods came, and the winds blew, and beat upon that house; and it fell not: for it was founded upon a rock. And every one that heareth these sayings of mine, and doeth them not, shall be likened unto a foolish man, which built his house upon the sand: And the rain descended, and the floods came, and the winds blew, and beat upon that house; and it fell: and great was the fall of it.

– Matthew 7:24–27

598. Roll the care of your day over on the Lord in prayer. You will still take necessary steps to address it. Yet, you won't be burdened down with worry or concern. You will access His wisdom. He will guide your thoughts to handle it.

Commit thy works unto the Lord, and thy thoughts shall be established.

– Proverbs 16:3

599. God will save anyone who calls on Him, if you are willing to obey Him, and believe on His Only Begotten Son,

Jesus Christ. Jesus died on the cross–to pay for our sins. They're paid in full. God then raised Jesus from the dead, so we could be free from eternal death. Just call on His name. Tell Him "l accept your payment Jesus" and you will be saved.

For whosoever shall call upon the name of the Lord shall be saved.

– Romans 10:13

600. You and I should be the kind of people that make such an impact on life and the cities we live in, that the reputation of the city will proclaim *"God is there!"*

It was round about eighteen thousand measures: and the name of the city from that day shall be, The Lord is there.

– Ezekiel 48:35

601. You can't stop the years, so you just have to make the most of them.

So teach us to number our days, that we may apply our hearts unto wisdom.

– Psalm 90:12

602. God will *"turn back time"* in order for you to get the miracle He has promised you. Just position yourself through obedience to His principles, and you can still obtain your destiny.

And Isaiah said, This sign shalt thou have of the Lord, that the Lord will do the thing that he hath spoken: shall the shadow go forward ten degrees, or go back ten degrees? And Hezekiah answered, It is a light thing for the shadow to go down ten degrees: nay, but let the shadow return backward ten degrees. And Isaiah the prophet cried unto the Lord: and he brought the shadow ten degrees backward, by which it had gone down in the dial of Ahaz.

–2 Kings 20:9–11

And I will restore to you the years that the locust hath eaten, the cankerworm, and the caterpiller, and the palmerworm, my great army which I sent among you. And ye shall eat in plenty, and be satisfied, and praise the name of the Lord your God, that hath dealt wondrously with you: and my people shall never be ashamed.

– Joel 2:25–26

Redeeming the time, because the days are evil.

– Ephesians 5:16

603. God's blessing is not *exclusive* to only a few. God promises to bless all who will diligently pursue His principles. The blessing is yours! *Go get it!*

Blessed is every one that feareth the Lord; that walketh in his ways. For thou shalt eat the labour of thine hands: happy shalt thou be, and it shall be well with thee.

– Psalm 128:1–2

604. God's Word works and it works every time. If we will be faithful to apply God's principles every time, we will obtain consistent success. God's Word is constant. Our faith is what *fluctuates.*

Heaven and earth shall pass away, but my words shall not pass away.

– Matthew 24:35

605. If you want some instant joy and strength, stop and take time to read three or four chapters of the Bible. You will find that *"the joy of the Lord is your strength!"* Also, listen to some praise and worship music!

Thy words were found, and I did eat them; and thy word was unto me the joy and rejoicing of mine heart: for I am called by thy name, O Lord God of hosts.

–Jeremiah 15:16

606. You can walk through life calm, confident, cool, and collected when you know you have *filled* your heart with God's way of doing things, through meditating His Word.

And I will walk at liberty: for I seek thy precepts.

–Psalm 119:45

607. It takes an alert mind to be inspired. To be ignited by a dream, goal, vision, or possibility is the first step toward any worthwhile accomplishment.

And the Lord answered me, and said, Write the vision, and make it plain upon tables, that he may run that readeth it. For the vision is yet for an appointed time, but at the end it shall speak, and not lie: though it tarry, wait for it; because it will surely come, it will not tarry. Behold, his soul, which is lifted up, is not upright in him: but the just shall live by his faith.

– Habakkuk 2:2–4

608. I'd rather be needed and liberal, than *stingy* and be in need.

There is that scattereth, and yet increaseth; and there is that withholdeth more than is meet, but it tendeth to poverty. The liberal soul shall be made fat: and he that watereth shall be watered also himself.

– Proverbs 11:24–25

609. People don't need you unless they need you, and if you don't help them when they need you, they don't *need you.*

If a brother or sister be naked, and destitute of daily food, And one of you say unto them, Depart in peace, be ye warmed and filled; notwithstanding ye give them not those things which are needful to the body; what doth it profit? Even so faith, if it hath not works, is dead, being alone.

– James 2:15–17

610. The stronger your sense of purpose equals a stronger sense of *self–love*, which leads to a stronger sense of self–discipline and self–preservation. But, when people don't have a sense of purpose, they lose all restraint.

Where there is no vision, the people perish: but he that keepeth the law, happy is he.

– Proverbs 29:18

611. It may take a *moment* of inspiration to conceive a dream. But, it may take years of perspiration to bring it to pass. It's the difference between the *"act"* of conceiving a child and the *duty* of raising a child. However, if we do not faint in the process, we will see the dream come to pass.

For a dream cometh through the multitude of business; and a fool's voice is known by multitude of words.

– Ecclesiastes 5:3

612. Envision your true destiny. Declare and decree ownership of it now, today. Announce and welcome it's arrival into your today. You will draw it to you. It will manifest and come to pass.

Thou shalt also decree a thing, and it shall be established unto thee: and the light shall shine upon thy ways.

– Job 22:28

613. God has lifetime blessing for you and I. He has *meantime* grace to help you on your journey today. Meantime grace will sustain you as you obtain lifetime blessing.

For this thing I besought the Lord thrice, that it might depart from me. And he said unto me, My grace is sufficient for thee: for my strength is made perfect in weakness. Most gladly therefore will I rather glory in my infirmities, that the power of Christ may rest upon me.

–2 Corinthians 12:8–9

614. God is sovereign over your enemies. He is sovereign over your life. You have nothing and no one to fear. You are precious in God's sight. He knows every detail about you and your life. Love God. Obey His Word. And *fear not!*

And fear not them, which kill the body, but are not able to kill the soul: but rather fear him, which is able to destroy both soul and body in hell. Are not two sparrows sold for a farthing? and one of them shall not fall on the ground without your Father. But the very hairs of your head are all numbered. Fear ye not therefore, ye are of more value than many sparrows.

– Matthew 10:28–31

615. For every complaint, there's a solution. Stop complaining, and be, find, or create the solution.

And when it was evening, his disciples came to him, saying, This is a desert place, and the time is now past; send the multitude away, that they may go into the villages, and buy themselves victuals. But Jesus said unto them, They need not depart; give ye them to eat. And they say unto him, We have here but five loaves, and two fishes. He said, Bring them hither to me. And he commanded the multitude to sit down on the grass, and took the five loaves, and the two fishes, and looking up to heaven, he blessed, and brake, and gave the loaves to his disciples, and the disciples to the multitude. And they did all eat, and were filled: and they took up of the fragments that remained twelve baskets full. And they that had eaten were about five thousand men, beside women and children.

– Matthew 14:15–21

616. There's no failure in advancement. Whether your progress is large or small, little or great, there's no failure as long as you keep on advancing.

In all labour there is profit: but the talk of the lips tendeth only to penury.

– Proverbs 14:23

617. Make yourself *indispensable* to your job and in life, by becoming a better servant of all. Serve right where you are. You will eventually be given responsibility to become ruler of all.

Who then is a faithful and wise servant, whom his lord hath made ruler over his household, to give them meat in due season? Blessed is that servant, whom his lord when he cometh shall find so doing. Verily I say unto you, That he shall make him ruler over all his goods.

– Matthew 24:45–47

618. There is no limit to what one life can do. One life who realizes their potential, and has the commitment to see that potential released. One life can change the world! One life can change generations. That one life is *yours!*

For if thou altogether holdest thy peace at this time, then shall there enlargement and deliverance arise to the Jews from another place; but thou and thy father's house shall be destroyed: and who knoweth whether thou art come to the kingdom for such a time as this?

– Esther 4:14

619. The only way to be remembered when you're gone is to make a significant contribution and impact while you're here!

For to him that is joined to all the living there is hope: for a living dog is better than a dead lion. For the living know that they shall die: but the dead know not any thing, neither have they any more a reward; for the memory of them is forgotten. Also their love, and their hatred, and their envy, is now perished; neither have they any more a portion for ever in any

thing that is done under the sun. Go thy way, eat thy bread with joy, and drink thy wine with a merry heart; for God now accepteth thy works. Let thy garments be always white; and let thy head lack no ointment. Live joyfully with the wife whom thou lovest all the days of the life of thy vanity, which he hath given thee under the sun, all the days of thy vanity: for that is thy portion in this life, and in thy labour which thou takest under the sun. Whatsoever thy hand findeth to do, do it with thy might; for there is no work, nor device, nor knowledge, nor wisdom, in the grave, whither thou goest. I returned, and saw under the sun, that the race is not to the swift, nor the battle to the strong, neither yet bread to the wise, nor yet riches to men of understanding, nor yet favour to men of skill; but time and chance happeneth to them all.

– Ecclesiastes 9:4–11

620. Attempts to bring intimidation and fear are foiled by bold resolve, dignity, and peace. Peace is a stronger weapon than intimidation and fear.

And in nothing terrified by your adversaries: which is to them an evident token of perdition, but to you of salvation, and that of God.

– Philippians 1:28

621. Neither terror at home nor terror abroad has the power to intimidate those who put their trust in God.

And in nothing terrified by your adversaries: which is to them an evident token of perdition, but to you of salvation, and that of God.

– Philippians 1:28

622. Just a word of encouragement: you are a champion! You have already won more battles than the average person. You have the crowns of victory. Be strong! Be bold! Be confident! Be calm, peaceful, cool, and collected. God is in you, with you, and for you! You're doing great! You've already overcome in life!

Ye are of God, little children, and have overcome them: because greater is he that is in you, than he that is in the world.

–1 John 4:4

623. Be thankful in this season for the bounty of blessings God has blessed your hands to obtain. There is nothing better than for a person to rejoice and be thankful for the bounty of blessing that God has blessed them with in life!

Wherefore I perceive that there is nothing better, than that a man should rejoice in his own works; for that is his portion: for who shall bring him to see what shall be after him?

–Ecclesiastes 3:22

624. If you are currently reading this, you officially have a reason to be thankful. Thank God for life, health, strength, safety, family, home, food, water, clothes, a sound mind, eyesight, hearing, speech, and appetite to enjoy that turkey! *Happy Thanksgiving!*

Then he said unto them, Go your way, eat the fat, and drink the sweet, and send portions unto them for whom nothing is prepared: for this day is holy unto our Lord: neither be ye sorry; for the joy of the Lord is your strength.

– Nehemiah 8:10

625. If you feel like you don't know clearly what the path is, don't be afraid–God does. Prayer and the Bible are the navigational tools in *"GPS (God's Positioning System!)"*.

Trust in the Lord with all thine heart; and lean not unto thine own understanding. In all thy ways acknowledge him, and he shall direct thy paths.

– Proverbs 3:5–6

626. Thanksgiving Day is a great day to officially give up the *habit* of complaining. Make it a resolution to live life thankfully each and everyday.

Rejoice in the Lord always: and again I say, Rejoice. Let your moderation be known unto all men. The Lord is at hand. Be careful for nothing; but in every thing by prayer and supplication with thanksgiving let your requests be made

known unto God. And the peace of God, which passeth all understanding, shall keep your hearts and minds through Christ Jesus. Finally, brethren, whatsoever things are true, whatsoever things are honest, whatsoever things are just, whatsoever things are pure, whatsoever things are lovely, whatsoever things are of good report; if there be any virtue, and if there be any praise, think on these things. Those things, which ye have both learned, and received, and heard, and seen in me, do: and the God of peace shall be with you.

– Philippians 4:4–9

627. You don't forgive and then forget the *experience.* Rather, you forgive and now you have new information as to what is possible from that person or persons. Yet, you free yourself from the shackles and poison of un–forgiveness.

Wherefore, though I wrote unto you, I did it not for his cause that had done the wrong, nor for his cause that suffered wrong, but that our care for you in the sight of God might appear unto you.

–2 Corinthians 7:12

628. The time and distance between offenses makes forgetting easier. The increase in love and wisdom between offenses makes forgiving easier.

The discretion of a man deferreth his anger; and it is his glory to pass over a transgression.

He that covereth a transgression seeketh love; but he that repeateth a matter separateth very friends.

– Proverbs 17:9

Only by pride cometh contention: but with the well advised is wisdom.

– Proverbs 13:10

629. Eventually people must realize that you are *one of a kind* and *one at a time*. You can please some of the people, some of the time, but you can't please all of the people, all of the time, at the same the time.

Brethren, I count not myself to have apprehended: but this one thing I do, forgetting those things which are behind, and reaching forth unto those things which are before, I press toward the mark for the prize of the high calling of God in Christ Jesus.

– Philippians 3:13–14

630. Don't let life *happen* to you, rather, you should happen to life. Planning and execution makes the difference.

Boast not thyself of to morrow; for thou knowest not what a day may bring forth.

– Proverbs 27:1

631. Everything's all right. And even if it's not all right, God can make it all right. It will be *all right!*

And we know that all things work together for good to them that love God, to them who are the called according to his purpose. For whom he did foreknow, he also did predestinate to be conformed to the image of his Son, that he might be the firstborn among many brethren.

– Romans 8:28–29

632. Whatever your challenge today, do not forget the *testimony* of your previous victories. The same God that delivered you before will deliver you now. The fact that you are still standing is evidence that you can overcome today.

And David said to Saul, Let no man's heart fail because of him; thy servant will go and fight with this Philistine. And Saul said to David, Thou art not able to go against this Philistine to fight with him: for thou art but a youth, and he a man of war from his youth. And David said unto Saul, Thy servant kept his father's sheep, and there came a lion, and a bear, and took a lamb out of the flock: And I went out after him, and smote him, and delivered it out of his mouth: and when he arose against me, I caught him by his beard, and smote him, and slew him. Thy servant slew both the lion and the bear: and this uncircumcised Philistine shall be as one of them, seeing he hath defied the armies of the living God.

–1 Samuel 17:32–36

633. You only succeed at what you *do*.

In all labour there is profit: but the talk of the lips tendeth only to penury.

– Proverbs 14:23

634. Once you learn *how* to learn, you can learn anything.

Wisdom is the principal thing; therefore get wisdom: and with all thy getting get understanding.

– Proverbs 4:7

635. Amazing grace! How sweet the sound that saved a man like me. How amazing is God's grace? I can't tell. All I know is that it was strong enough to rescue my soul from *Hell!* Jesus is still the answer for the world today!

Be it known unto you all, and to all the people of Israel, that by the name of Jesus Christ of Nazareth, whom ye crucified, whom God raised from the dead, *even* by him doth this man stand here before you whole. This is the stone, which was set at nought of you builders, which is become the head of the corner. Neither is there salvation in any other: for there is none other name under heaven given among men, whereby we must be saved.

– Acts 4:10–12

636. God is your shield today against all adversity. He will uphold you from evil. He will keep you from the plots of the enemy. You are God's top priority today. Call on His name, Jesus! He will help and save you this very day! Be strong and depend on His name!

God is our refuge and strength, a very present help in trouble.

– Psalm 46:1

637. A lie is only for a season, but truth shall stand for eternity.

The lip of truth shall be established for ever: but a lying tongue is but for a moment.

– Proverbs 12:19

638. God can help us to transcend the negative realities that seek to assassinate our futures. Internal ascension; proceeds external elevation.

And Jabez was more honourable than his brethren: and his mother called his name Jabez, saying, Because I bare him with sorrow. And Jabez called on the God of Israel, saying, Oh that thou wouldest bless me indeed, and enlarge my coast, and that thine hand might be with me, and that thou wouldest keep me from evil, that it may not grieve me! And God granted him that which he requested.

–1 Chronicles 4:9–10

639. Be sure to take time daily, to enjoy the sunshine, because you can't buy it in a bottle. You must enjoy it, *one day at time!*

So teach us to number our days, that we may apply our hearts unto wisdom.

– Psalm 90:12

640. Many people operate under a premise of misguided conceit, and the undervaluing of the dignity of others. This leads to failure, separation, and misunderstanding.

Honour all men. Love the brotherhood. Fear God. Honour the king.

–1 Peter 2:17

641. Most people don't spend enough time with themselves to *recognize* themselves. You must spend enough time with yourself to recognize your own value.

But let every man prove his own work, and then shall he have rejoicing in himself alone, and not in another.

– Galatians 6:4

642. Trust your ability to be creative. Make known those things that are not yet known. Bring them into reality.

Now faith is the substance of things hoped for, the evidence of things not seen. For by it the elders obtained a good report.

Through faith we understand that the worlds were framed by the word of God, so that things, which are seen, were not made of things, which do appear.

– Hebrews 11:1–3

643. Most people's thoughts reflect the thoughts of others. Often, they haven't taken time to celebrate their own thoughts, nor value them. You can trust your own ability to think. You were made in the image and likeness of God. You have the mind of Christ. The thoughts of the righteous are right!

The thoughts of the righteous are right: but the counsels of the wicked are deceit.

– Proverbs 12:5

644. If God has changed the world with anyone, He can change the world with anyone! He can use *you!*

I can do all things through Christ, which strengtheneth me.

– Philippians 4:13

645. Trim all the *"fat"* out of your life, and focus on what actually needs to get done. Stop wasting time. Stop complaining. And make what needs to happen, happen! You can do it!

I can do all things through Christ, which strengtheneth me.

– Philippians 4:13

646. If you just focus on doing what needs to get done, you will get a *whole lot* done!

In all labour there is profit: but the talk of the lips tendeth only to penury.

– Proverbs 14:23

647. Someone is *observing* your diligence and work ethic. It will be the key to your promotion and reward in life.

Then said Boaz unto his servant that was set over the reapers, Whose damsel is this? And the servant that was set over the reapers answered and said, It is the Moabitish damsel that came back with Naomi out of the country of Moab: And she said, I pray you, let me glean and gather after the reapers among the sheaves: so she came, and hath continued even from the morning until now, that she tarried a little in the house.

– Ruth 2:5–7

648. God's Word works every time that you work it. There's no lack of power in the Word, there's only a lack of diligence to use it. Pray Psalm 91 over you and your family for protection and to bind the devil.

He that dwelleth in the secret place of the most High shall abide under the shadow of the Almighty. I will say of

the Lord, He is my refuge and my fortress: my God; in him will I trust. Surely he shall deliver thee from the snare of the fowler, and from the noisome pestilence. He shall cover thee with his feathers, and under his wings shalt thou trust: his truth shall be thy shield and buckler. Thou shalt not be afraid for the terror by night; nor for the arrow that flieth by day; Nor for the pestilence that walketh in darkness; nor for the destruction that wasteth at noonday. A thousand shall fall at thy side, and ten thousand at thy right hand; but it shall not come nigh thee. Only with thine eyes shalt thou behold and see the reward of the wicked. Because thou hast made the Lord, which is my refuge, even the most High, thy habitation; There shall no evil befall thee, neither shall any plague come nigh thy dwelling. For he shall give his angels charge over thee, to keep thee in all thy ways. They shall bear thee up in their hands, lest thou dash thy foot against a stone. Thou shalt tread upon the lion and adder: the young lion and the dragon shalt thou trample under feet. Because he hath set his love upon me, therefore will I deliver him: I will set him on high, because he hath known my name. He shall call upon me, and I will answer him: I will be with him in trouble; I will deliver him, and honour him. With long life will I satisfy him, and shew him my salvation.

–Psalm 91

649. Give thanks for a brand new day! Be thankful for the ability to see, walk, talk, think, eat, work, pray, play, love, give, laugh, and live! Take time to give God thanks for *life* today!

It is a good thing to give thanks unto the Lord, and to sing praises unto thy name, O Most High: To shew forth thy lovingkindness in the morning, and thy faithfulness every night.

– Psalm 92:1–2

650. *God* is God, and you are not! Just because you don't know what's going on, doesn't mean that God is not in control. He's God, and you are not!

Behold, I go forward, but he is not there; and backward, but I cannot perceive him: On the left hand, where he doth work, but I cannot behold him: he hideth himself on the right hand, that I cannot see him: But he knoweth the way that I take: when he hath tried me, I shall come forth as gold.

– Job 23:8–10

651. In life, *ain't nothing happening* unless you happen!

For as the body without the spirit is dead, so faith without works is dead also.

– James 2:26

652. Make your own favor! Do the same things that were done by those you perceive to be your sources of favor, and you will get the same results. God's favor is attached to universal principles. It's free to all!

Pastor Terrance Levise Turner

Seest thou a man diligent in his business? he shall stand before kings; he shall not stand before mean men.

– Proverbs 22:29

653. You don't need someone else's *permission* to be great. All you need is willingness and competence.

Now therefore perform the doing of it; that as there was a readiness to will, so there may be a performance also out of that which ye have. For if there be first a willing mind, it is accepted according to that a man hath, and not according to that he hath not.

–2 Corinthians 8:11–12

654. There are seven billion people, and a big, big world out there! You don't need favor with everyone; you only need favor with *someone*. Just do what God gave you to do. God will bless you.

Now therefore perform the doing of it; that as there was a readiness to will, so there may be a performance also out of that which ye have. For if there be first a willing mind, it is accepted according to that a man hath, and not according to that he hath not.

–2 Corinthians 8:11–12

655. Prayer is a seed. The Word is a seed. If you consistently plant the word of faith in prayer, plus action, you

will get the harvest of what you planted. Just like planting the seed of corn produces the harvest of corn in the process of time.

And he said, So is the kingdom of God, as if a man should cast seed into the ground; And should sleep, and rise night and day, and the seed should spring and grow up, he knoweth not how. For the earth bringeth forth fruit of herself; first the blade, then the ear, after that the full corn in the ear. But when the fruit is brought forth, immediately he putteth in the sickle, because the harvest is come.

– Mark 4:26–29

656. Sometimes prayer is to deliver you *"from"*, but most times it's to deliver you *"through"*.

Yea, though I walk through the valley of the shadow of death, I will fear no evil: for thou art with me; thy rod and thy staff they comfort me.

– Psalm 23:4

657. If you'll compromise on small things, you'll compromise on big things.

Take us the foxes, the little foxes, that spoil the vines: for our vines have tender grapes.

– Song of Solomon 2:15

658. On the journey of success you have to continue to take steps and trust God in the process. You will see your harvest.

The steps of a good man are ordered by the Lord: and he delighteth in his way.

– Psalm 37:23

659. Don't be afraid to start that business. God can trust you to manage your own time. God can trust you to be diligent. God can trust you to be your *own* taskmaster.

Go to the ant, thou sluggard; consider her ways, and be wise: which having no guide, overseer, or ruler, provideth her meat in the summer, and gathereth her food in the harvest.

– Proverbs 6:6–8

660. Only the person who *made* themselves, keeps themselves alive, keeps their own heart beating, keeps their own mind sane, made their own planet, made their own air...has room to *boast* in God's world!

O the depth of the riches both of the wisdom and knowledge of God! How unsearchable are his judgments, and his ways past finding out! For who hath known the mind of the Lord? or who hath been his counsellor? Or who hath first given to him, and it shall be recompensed unto him again? For of him, and through him, and to him, are all things: to whom be glory forever. Amen.

– Romans 11:33–36

661. I can still breathe even if someone else is holding his or her breath. I won't let another person's bitterness control my happiness!

But the father said to his servants, Bring forth the best robe, and put it on him; and put a ring on his hand, and shoes on his feet: And bring hither the fatted calf, and kill it; and let us eat, and be merry: For this my son was dead, and is alive again; he was lost, and is found. And they began to be merry. Now his elder son was in the field: and as he came and drew nigh to the house, he heard musick and dancing. And he called one of the servants, and asked what these things meant. And he said unto him, Thy brother is come; and thy father hath killed the fatted calf, because he hath received him safe and sound. And he was angry, and would not go in: therefore came his father out, and intreated him. And he answering said to his father, Lo, these many years do I serve thee, neither transgressed I at any time thy commandment: and yet thou never gavest me a kid, that I might make merry with my friends: But as soon as this thy son was come, which hath devoured thy living with harlots, thou hast killed for him the fatted calf. And he said unto him, Son, thou art ever with me, and all that I have is thine. It was meet that we should make merry, and be glad: for this thy brother was dead, and is alive again; and was lost, and is found.

– Luke 15:22–32

662. At this time in life we must be intentionally merry for Christmas, while remaining responsibly sober. We must make the choice to enjoy the celebration, while remaining vigilant regarding the world in which we live.

Then he said unto them, Go your way, eat the fat, and drink the sweet, and send portions unto them for whom nothing is prepared: for this day is holy unto our Lord: neither be ye sorry; for the joy of the Lord is your strength.

– Nehemiah 8:10

663. In the midst of all of life's high intensity circumstances, it's good to have the occasional *"decaf moment"* –the kind that doesn't add to the drama!

Thou wilt keep him in perfect peace, whose mind is stayed on thee: because he trusteth in thee. Trust ye in the Lord for ever: for in the Lord JEHOVAH is everlasting strength:

– Isaiah 26:3–4

664. When you love God, even things that seem unplanned and unpleasant can be turned around for your good. He's still sovereign. He holds the world in the palm of His hand. He has power to *turn it around*!

And we know that all things work together for good to them that love God, to them who are the called according to his purpose. For whom he did foreknow, he also did predestinate

to be conformed to the image of his Son, that he might be the firstborn among many brethren.

– Romans 8:28–29

665. A leader is who *will*.

Now therefore perform the doing of it; that as there was a readiness to will, so there may be a performance also out of that which ye have. For if there be first a willing mind, it is accepted according to that a man hath, and not according to that he hath not.

–2 Corinthians 8:11–12

666. May you be endued with favor from on high. May your family be prosperous this Christmas. May all God's blessings surround you and yours. May God's peace rest upon all nations this Christmas season.

For unto you is born this day in the city of David a Saviour, which is Christ the Lord. And this *shall be a* sign unto you; Ye shall find the babe wrapped in swaddling clothes, lying in a manger. And suddenly there was with the angel a multitude of the heavenly host praising God, and saying, Glory to God in the highest, and on earth peace, good will toward men.

– Luke 2:11–14

667. Sometimes it's not all about the presents. Sometimes miracles are just in the *presence*. Be sure to spend time with

your family and friends celebrating the joy, love, and peace of Christmas this year!

And the angel said unto them, Fear not: for, behold, I bring you good tidings of great joy, which shall be to all people. For unto you is born this day in the city of David a Saviour, which is Christ the Lord. And this shall be a sign unto you; Ye shall find the babe wrapped in swaddling clothes, lying in a manger. And suddenly there was with the angel a multitude of the heavenly host praising God, and saying, Glory to God in the highest, and on earth peace, good will toward men. And it came to pass, as the angels were gone away from them into heaven, the shepherds said one to another, Let us now go even unto Bethlehem, and see this thing which is come to pass, which the Lord hath made known unto us. And they came with haste, and found Mary, and Joseph, and the babe lying in a manger.

– Luke 2:10–16

668. Sustainable, replicable blessings are not based on miracles. They are based on *principles*. You can tell your children about your miracles, but you must *teach* them your success principles.

And the manna ceased on the morrow after they had eaten of the old corn of the land; neither had the children of Israel manna any more; but they did eat of the fruit of the land of Canaan that year.

– Joshua 5:12

669. It takes a special capacity, tenacity, and audacity to be rich. Those who possess it have the greatest chance of accomplishing it!

The crown of the wise is their riches: but the foolishness of fools is folly.

– Proverbs 14:24

670. If it seems wrong, *it is.*

And they which heard it, being convicted by their own conscience, went out one by one, beginning at the eldest, even unto the last: and Jesus was left alone, and the woman standing in the midst.

– John 8:9

671. Due to all the unscheduled events that can happen, you need to learn to take life with a *"chill pill!"* And have a Merry Christmas celebration!

Rejoice in the Lord alway: and again I say, Rejoice. Let your moderation be known unto all men. The Lord is at hand. Be careful for nothing; but in every thing by prayer and supplication with thanksgiving let your requests be made known unto God. And the peace of God, which passeth all understanding, shall keep your hearts and minds through Christ Jesus. Finally, brethren, whatsoever things are true, whatsoever things are honest, whatsoever things are just, whatsoever things are pure, whatsoever things are lovely,

whatsoever things are of good report; if there be any virtue, and if there be any praise, think on these things. Those things, which ye have both learned, and received, and heard, and seen in me, do: and the God of peace shall be with you.

– Philippians 4:4–9

672. The same Jesus you believed in, read about, and heard about as a child, is the same Jesus we are to celebrate this Christmas season. Don't allow your heart to be misled by the media or society's disrespect of that holy name. It took calling on *Jesus* to save you–it will take Him to take you to heaven when He comes!

And that from a child thou hast known the holy scriptures, which are able to make thee wise unto salvation through faith which is in Christ Jesus.

–2 Timothy 3:15

673. Often the greatest gifts are misunderstood or perhaps overlooked. Yet, God often works in mysterious ways to bring us the gifts that will enrich our lives the most. Merry Christmas to you! As we celebrate and accept the *gift* of Jesus, God's Holy Son!

Now the birth of Jesus Christ was on this wise: When as his mother Mary was espoused to Joseph, before they came together, she was found with child of the Holy Ghost. Then Joseph her husband, being a just man, and not willing to make her a public example, was minded to put her away privily. But

while he thought on these things, behold, the angel of the Lord appeared unto him in a dream, saying, Joseph, thou son of David, fear not to take unto thee Mary thy wife: for that which is conceived in her is of the Holy Ghost. And she shall bring forth a son, and thou shalt call his name Jesus: for he shall save his people from their sins.

– Matthew 1:18–21

674. Whatever may be your challenge, and whatever may be your impossible situation, I want you to know that God *specializes* in impossible circumstances–that's why Jesus came on Christmas day!

For with God nothing shall be impossible.

– Luke 1:37

675. What's more reliable, miracles or principles? What's more controllable, miracles or principles? Both. Work the principles, and thus position yourself as a candidate for the *miracle.*

In the morning sow thy seed, and in the evening withhold not thine hand: for thou knowest not whether shall prosper, either this or that, or whether they both shall be alike good.

– Ecclesiastes 11:6

676. Many people don't know God in His ways. They only have an image of who they think or desire Him to be.

However, the true worshippers of God must worship Him in spirit and in truth.

Jesus saith unto her, Woman, believe me, the hour cometh, when ye shall neither in this mountain, nor yet at Jerusalem, worship the Father. Ye worship ye know not what: we know what we worship: for salvation is of the Jews. But the hour cometh, and now is, when the true worshippers shall worship the Father in spirit and in truth: for the Father seeketh such to worship him. God is a Spirit: and they that worship him must worship him in spirit and in truth.

– John 4:21–24

677. The truth is not always about being *positive*: the truth is about always being *positively true*. Preaching is not always about being motivational: preaching is about always motivating us to *change*.

All scripture is given by inspiration of God, and is profitable for doctrine, for reproof, for correction, for instruction in righteousness.

–2 Timothy 3:16

678. Seek daily to live on purpose, rather than only working for a living. This is the key to happiness, wealth, and joy! Merry Christmas!

Wherefore I perceive that there is nothing better, than that a man should rejoice in his own works; for that is his portion: for who shall bring him to see what shall be after him?

– Ecclesiastes 3:22

679. Most relationships are based on a *"point system"*. Therefore, you might as well face it and learn how to *shoot!* Because the question will always be *"what have you done for me lately?"*

Give, and it shall be given unto you; good measure, pressed down, and shaken together, and running over, shall men give into your bosom. For with the same measure that ye mete withal it shall be measured to you again.

– Luke 6:38

680. The prescription for most of life's situations is: keep working in excellence, and keep walking in love. Excellence can't be spoken against, and love wins overall.

Seest thou a man diligent in his business? he shall stand before kings; he shall not stand before mean men.

– Proverbs 22:29

And now abideth faith, hope, charity, these three; but the greatest of these is charity.

–1 Corinthians 13:13

681. The same God that caused you to eat *everyday:* is the same God that will cause you to eat *everyday.*

Give us this day our daily bread.

– Matthew 6:11

682. God, our Heavenly Father wishes above all things that we *grow–up*, mature, and take responsibility to manage life successfully. To walk in love and responsibility is the sign of godly maturity.

Brethren, be not children in understanding: howbeit in malice be ye children, but in understanding be men.

–1 Corinthians 14:20

683. Often it takes the innocence of a little child to remind us of the most important things in life. May you have the *faith of a child* this Christmas, and receive God's greatest *gift*, Jesus Christ, His Holy Son, by faith.

The wolf also shall dwell with the lamb, and the leopard shall lie down with the kid; and the calf and the young lion and the fatling together; and a little child shall lead them.

– Isaiah 11:6

684. In life, you have to be able to navigate within the narrow–view, which is mankind's view, and the wide–view, which is God's view. We see what's right in front of us, but

God sees the entire, infinite view. Take care of the immediate; but trust God for the eternal.

While we look not at the things which are seen, but at the things which are not seen: for the things which are seen are temporal; but the things which are not seen are eternal.

–2 Corinthians 4:18

685. Give honor to whom honor is due.

Honour all men. Love the brotherhood. Fear God. Honour the king.

–1 Peter 2:17

Render therefore to all their dues: tribute to whom tribute is due; custom to whom custom; fear to whom fear; honour to whom honour.

– Romans 13:7

686. We often take so many things for granted regarding God's grace and protection during perilous weather and other catastrophes. However, the grace of protection is an unmerited *gift* every time.

The angel of the Lord encampeth round about them that fear him, and delivereth them.

– Psalm 34:7

687. Someone else's need is your opportunity to sow a seed toward your future. If you refuse to sow to meet someone else's need, you neglect the future harvest that you will need someday soon. Merry Christmas!

But by an equality, that now at this time your abundance may be a supply for their want, that their abundance also may be a supply for your want: that there may be equality: As it is written, He that had gathered much had nothing over; and he that had gathered little had no lack.

–2 Corinthians 8: 14–15

688. If we will control, what we can control we will control everything. Exercise, eat right, get rest, get up earlier, read information and knowledge, make a budget, etc. Control what you can and you will control *everything*.

This I say then, Walk in the Spirit, and ye shall not fulfil the lust of the flesh. For the flesh lusteth against the Spirit, and the Spirit against the flesh: and these are contrary the one to the other: so that ye cannot do the things that ye would. But if ye be led of the Spirit, ye are not under the law.

– Galatians 5:16–18

689. Sometimes too much support can be crippling. You don't need a *cane* if you're not cripple.

But when it pleased God, who separated me from my mother's womb, and called me by his grace, to reveal his Son

in me, that I might preach him among the heathen; immediately I conferred not with flesh and blood: neither went I up to Jerusalem to them which were apostles before me; but I went into Arabia, and returned again unto Damascus. Then after three years I went up to Jerusalem to see Peter, and abode with him fifteen days. But other of the apostles saw I none, save James the Lord's brother.

– Galatians 1:15–19

690. We often pray for patience, but patience takes time and testing.

Knowing this, that the trying of your faith worketh patience. But let patience have her perfect work, that ye may be perfect and entire, wanting nothing. If any of you lack wisdom, let him ask of God, that giveth to all men liberally, and upbraideth not; and it shall be given him.

– James 1:3–5

691. As you start each day, leave no space for the Devil. Leave no space of your life *"void"* of the Word of God. Speak the Word only!

Neither give place to the devil.

–Ephesians 4:27

In the beginning God created the heaven and the earth. And the earth was without form, and void; and darkness was upon the face of the deep. And the Spirit of God moved upon the

face of the waters. And God said, Let there be light: and there was light. And God saw the light, that it was good: and God divided the light from the darkness.

–Genesis 1:1–4

The centurion answered and said, Lord, I am not worthy that thou shouldest come under my roof: but speak the word only, and my servant shall be healed.

– Matthew 8:8

692. Turn your heart in repentance to God. He will forgive. He will deliver. He is merciful. He is gracious. He is married to the backslider.

Take with you words, and turn to the Lord: say unto him, Take away all iniquity, and receive us graciously: so will we render the calves of our lips. Asshur shall not save us; we will not ride upon horses: neither will we say any more to the work of our hands, Ye are our gods: for in thee the fatherless findeth mercy. I will heal their backsliding, I will love them freely: for mine anger is turned away from him.

– Hosea 14:2–4

693. The *"Cross"* is still the *true* reason for this season. Jesus came on Christmas Day in order to die on the cross 33 years later to pay for our sins. God raised Him from the dead after three days, to give us eternal life. Please accept God's only Christmas *Gift* for the entire world today.

For God so loved the world, that he gave his only begotten Son, that whosoever believeth in him should not perish, but have everlasting life. For God sent not his Son into the world to condemn the world; but that the world through him might be saved

– John 3:16–17

694. The key to distinction and preference on your job, in business, and in life, will be your possession of an excellent, faithful spirit and disposition. Who you are on the inside, will determine your success and promotion on the outside.

Then this Daniel was preferred above the presidents and princes, because an excellent spirit was in him; and the king thought to set him over the whole realm.

– Daniel 6:3

Mark the perfect man, and behold the upright: for the end of that man is peace.

– Psalm 37:37

695. Daily we are faced with the decision of what we will focus on. We are presented with multiple images, advertisements, and enticements; however, only we have control of what we dwell and meditate upon. It will determine our success or downfall.

I will set no wicked thing before mine eyes: I hate the work of them that turn aside; it shall not cleave to me.

– Psalm 101:3

696. The sexual urge is the most natural behavior between a man and a woman. God gave it, for our enjoyment and for procreation. However, the Creator set the parameters, to be within marriage.

Nevertheless, to avoid fornication, let every man have his own wife, and let every woman have her own husband.

–1 Corinthians 7:2

697. Some people judge a whole story based on a season, yet even a year has *four* seasons.

The steps of a good man are ordered by the Lord: and he delighteth in his way. Though he fall, he shall not be utterly cast down: for the Lord upholdeth him with his hand.

– Psalm 37:23–25

For a just man falleth seven times, and riseth up again: but the wicked shall fall into mischief.

– Proverbs 24:16

698. Being prompt to appointments, is a sign of *consideration* and love for other people. Lateness is an expression of lack of consideration and respect, or a lack of responsibility and self-management.

Let nothing be done through strife or vainglory; but in lowliness of mind let each esteem other better than themselves. Look not every man on his own things, but every man also on the things of others.

– Philippians 2:3–4

So teach us to number our days, that we may apply our hearts unto wisdom.

– Psalm 90:12

699. Don't worry: pray. Prayer *travels*.

Confess your faults one to another, and pray one for another, that ye may be healed. The effectual fervent prayer of a righteous man availeth much. Elias was a man subject to like passions as we are, and he prayed earnestly that it might not rain: and it rained not on the earth by the space of three years and six months. And he prayed again, and the heaven gave rain, and the earth brought forth her fruit.

– James 5:16–18

700. People don't succeed because they *want to*; people succeed because they *work to!*

For as the body without the spirit is dead, so faith without works is dead also.

– James 2:26

Seest thou a man diligent in his business? he shall stand before kings; he shall not stand before mean men.

– Proverbs 22:29

In all labour there is profit: but the talk of the lips tendeth only to penury.

–Proverbs 14:23

701. It's not perfect. But, it's *done!*

In all labour there is profit: but the talk of the lips tendeth only to penury.

– Proverbs 14:23

702. It's not always what's said, that's being said. Often it's what's *unsaid*, that's really being said.

He that answereth a matter before he heareth it, it is folly and shame unto him.

– Proverbs 18:13

The simple believeth every word: but the prudent man looketh well to his going.

– Proverbs 14:15

703. Everything that I am and all that I will be, I owe unequivocally to my mother getting to know Jesus, and

choosing to live a life that introduced me to Him. All the good that I am, is because of Jesus. May you know Him this year. Happy New Year!

Praise ye the Lord. Praise, O ye servants of the Lord, praise the name of the Lord. Blessed be the name of the Lord from this time forth and for evermore. From the rising of the sun unto the going down of the same the Lord's name is to be praised. The Lord is high above all nations, and his glory above the heavens. Who is like unto the Lord our God, who dwelleth on high, Who humbleth himself to behold the things that are in heaven, and in the earth! He raiseth up the poor out of the dust, and lifteth the needy out of the dunghill; That he may set him with princes, even with the princes of his people. He maketh the barren woman to keep house, and to be a joyful mother of children. Praise ye the Lord.

– Psalm 113

704. Whatever you may have faced this year, know for sure that *God is still in charge* of your life. When your life is in God's hands, He leaves no area untouched!

There hath no temptation taken you but such as is common to man: but God is faithful, who will not suffer you to be tempted above that ye are able; but will with the temptation also make a way to escape, that ye may be able to bear it.

–1 Corinthians 10:13

705. Sometimes you have to *let* a day happen, in order to get the hidden treasures that God has placed in that day. Don't *fight* every unscheduled event.

A man's heart deviseth his way: but the Lord directeth his steps.

– Proverbs 16:9

The lot is cast into the lap; but the whole disposing thereof is of the Lord.

– Proverbs 16:33

706. Whatever you may be facing, please *hasten to God's throne*! He will hear you. He will answer you. He will comfort you.

For the word of God is quick, and powerful, and sharper than any twoedged sword, piercing even to the dividing asunder of soul and spirit, and of the joints and marrow, and is a discerner of the thoughts and intents of the heart. Neither is there any creature that is not manifest in his sight: but all things are naked and opened unto the eyes of him with whom we have to do. Seeing then that we have a great high priest, that is passed into the heavens, Jesus the Son of God, let us hold fast our profession. For we have not an high priest which cannot be touched with the feeling of our infirmities; but was in all points tempted like as we are, yet without sin. Let us therefore come boldly unto the throne of grace, that we may obtain mercy, and find grace to help in time of need.

Distinguished Wisdom Presents . . . "Living Proverbs"–Vol.2

– Hebrews 4:12–16

707. Words and actions of carnality bring forth dead results. Words and actions of the *born–again* spirit bring forth the living, life–giving *"fruit of the spirit!"*

Now the works of the flesh are manifest, which are these; Adultery, fornication, uncleanness, lasciviousness, Idolatry, witchcraft, hatred, variance, emulations, wrath, strife, seditions, heresies, Envyings, murders, drunkenness, revellings, and such like: of the which I tell you before, as I have also told you in time past, that they which do such things shall not inherit the kingdom of God. But the fruit of the Spirit is love, joy, peace, longsuffering, gentleness, goodness, faith, Meekness, temperance: against such there is no law. And they that are Christ's have crucified the flesh with the affections and lusts. If we live in the Spirit, let us also walk in the Spirit.

– Galatians 5:19–25

708. As we start the New Year, may we recognize God's sovereignty over our lives and the world. He made us, and the world, and everyone in it. He is sovereign. His Word prevails over all of the dark, void, disorderly places of your life. Speak the Word *only* this year!

In the beginning God created the heaven and the earth. And the earth was without form, and void; and darkness was upon the face of the deep. And the Spirit of God moved upon the face of the waters. And God said, Let there be light: and there

was light. And God saw the light, that it was good: and God divided the light from the darkness.

– Genesis 1:1–4

The centurion answered and said, Lord, I am not worthy that thou shouldest come under my roof: but speak the word only, and my servant shall be healed.

– Matthew 8:8

709. Sometimes it's not about doing everything; rather, it's about doing *something*. Do something toward your annual, monthly, weekly, and daily goals everyday this year. You'll be pleasantly surprised at your *cumulative* progress!

In all labour there is profit: but the talk of the lips tendeth only to penury.

– Proverbs 14:23

So teach us to number our days, that we may apply our hearts unto wisdom.

– Psalm 90:12

710. If you can find God's Word on it, you can believe and strive for it! Believe God for a *biblical lifespan*. That's His plan for you. Change your mental and emotional perspective regarding life. Inwardly *reset* the limits in accordance with God's plan.

And the Lord said, My spirit shall not always strive with man, for that he also is flesh: yet his days shall be an hundred and twenty years.

— Genesis 6:3

711. If you can think of it, *it's yours!*

For as he thinketh in his heart, so is he...

— Proverbs 23:7a

The thoughts of the righteous are right...

— Proverbs 12:5a

I can do all things through Christ which strengtheneth me.

— Philippians 4:13

For with God nothing shall be impossible.

— Luke 1:37

712. God is not waiting on you to become *perfect* for you to succeed. Just go ahead and succeed and God will be *quite happy!*

Beloved, I wish above all things that thou mayest prosper and be in health, even as thy soul prospereth.

—3 John 1:2

Let them shout for joy, and be glad, that favour my righteous cause: yea, let them say continually, Let the Lord be magnified, which hath pleasure in the prosperity of his servant.

– Psalm 35:27

713. The time to *confess* is when you've done something that God can *bless!*

A man shall be satisfied with good by the fruit of his mouth: and the recompence of a man's hands shall be rendered unto him.

– Proverbs 12:14

714. Most people live with no sense of *aim*; therefore, they become aimless. Goals, purpose, and a vision are the keys to success.

Where there is no vision, the people perish: but he that keepeth the law, happy is he.

– Proverbs 29:18

715. May your life be enriched by the words of *wisdom.*

And how I kept back nothing that was profitable unto you, but have shewed you, and have taught you publicly, and from house to house.

– Acts 20:20

716. May your life enrich the earth through you contributing your *unforgettable gift*. Some treasures will be remembered forever.

As every man hath received the gift, even so minister the same one to another, as good stewards of the manifold grace of God.

–1 Peter 4:10

717. To exercise is a matter of *life*. To not exercise is a matter of *death*. It's a matter of life or death. Choose life!

Know ye not that they which run in a race run all, but one receiveth the prize? So run, that ye may obtain. And every man that striveth for the mastery is temperate in all things. Now they do it to obtain a corruptible crown; but we an incorruptible. I therefore so run, not as uncertainly; so fight I, not as one that beateth the air: But I keep under my body, and bring it into subjection: lest that by any means, when I have preached to others, I myself should be a castaway.

–1 Corinthians 9:24–27

718. You can't do your best, if you don't get your *rest*. You can't be the right size, if you don't exercise. You can't lead, if you don't read. You can't be raised, if you don't praise!

It is vain for you to rise up early, to sit up late, to eat the bread of sorrows: for so he giveth his beloved sleep.

−Psalms 126:2

But I keep under my body, and bring it into subjection: lest that by any means, when I have preached to others, I myself should be a castaway.

−1 Corinthians 9:27

Wisdom is the principal thing; therefore get wisdom: and with all thy getting get understanding.

−Proverbs 4:7

Humble yourselves therefore under the mighty hand of God, that he may exalt you in due time.

−1 Peter 5:6

719. You loving *you*, is you loving *me*, because if you don't love you, there will be no you for me to love!

Jesus said unto him, Thou shalt love the Lord thy God with all thy heart, and with all thy soul, and with all thy mind. This is the first and great commandment. And the second is like unto it, Thou shalt love thy neighbour as thyself. On these two commandments hang all the law and the prophets.

− Matthew 22:37–40

720. To help people in life: don't meddle rather *model*.

Not for that we have dominion over your faith, but are helpers of your joy: for by faith ye stand.

-2 Corinthians 1:24

Let no man despise thy youth; but be thou an example of the believers, in word, in conversation, in charity, in spirit, in faith, in purity.

-1 Timothy 4:12

721. Keep setting goals. Don't be afraid to set goals. Goals are achievable. Delays are what are unnatural, but goals are achievable. You were created to set and achieve your goals.

Where there is no vision, the people perish: but he that keepeth the law, happy is he.

– Proverbs 29:18

Thou shalt also decree a thing, and it shall be established unto thee: and the light shall shine upon thy ways.

– Job 22:28

Declaring the end from the beginning, and from ancient times the things that are not yet done, saying, My counsel shall stand, and I will do all my pleasure:

– Isaiah 46:10

And the Lord answered me, and said, Write the vision, and make it plain upon tables, that he may run that readeth it. For

the vision is yet for an appointed time, but at the end it shall speak, and not lie: though it tarry, wait for it; because it will surely come, it will not tarry. Behold, his soul which is lifted up is not upright in him: but the just shall live by his faith.

– Habakkuk 2:2–4

722. Fight *failure*! Success is the natural state of every person made in the image and likeness of God. Fight failure. It is *unnatural*.

And God said, Let us make man in our image, after our likeness: and let them have dominion over the fish of the sea, and over the fowl of the air, and over the cattle, and over all the earth, and over every creeping thing that creepeth upon the earth. So God created man in his own image, in the image of God created he him; male and female created he them. And God blessed them, and God said unto them, Be fruitful, and multiply, and replenish the earth, and subdue it: and have dominion over the fish of the sea, and over the fowl of the air, and over every living thing that moveth upon the earth.

– Genesis 1:26–28

723. May Jesus change your life in such a way this year that they that knew you in a *weaker* state will no longer recognize you. You once were blind, but now you *see!*

The neighbours therefore, and they which before had seen him that he was blind, said, Is not this he that sat and begged? Some said, This is he: others said, He is like him: but he said, I

am he. Therefore said they unto him, How were thine eyes opened? He answered and said, A man that is called Jesus made clay, and anointed mine eyes, and said unto me, Go to the pool of Siloam, and wash: and I went and washed, and I received sight.

– John 9:8–11

724. Meditate God's Word daily. May it be your continual source of peace and counsel. Let it be your source of daily success.

Seven times a day do I praise thee because of thy righteous judgments. Great peace have they which love thy law: and nothing shall offend them.

– Psalm 119:164–165

But his delight is in the law of the Lord; and in his law doth he meditate day and night. And he shall be like a tree planted by the rivers of water, that bringeth forth his fruit in his season; his leaf also shall not wither; and whatsoever he doeth shall prosper.

– Psalm 1:2–3

725. Your situation is not who you are. You are made in the image and likeness of God. A weaker man may cage a *lion*, yet man could never take away the majesty of such a mighty creature. And man better not leave that cage door open! Or he will learn why the lion *roars!*

The wicked flee when no man pursueth: but the righteous are bold as a lion.

– Proverbs 28:1

726. God wants you to take care of what needs to be done without taking the *care* of what needs to be done.

Humble yourselves therefore under the mighty hand of God, that he may exalt you in due time: Casting all your care upon him; for he careth for you.

–1 Peter 5:6–7

727. In most business and personal relationships, there is the tendency to downplay the value of what the other person has to offer, in order to *cheapen* the asking price. However, the way of God is to *esteem* others better than you.

It is naught, it is naught, saith the buyer: but when he is gone his way, then he boasteth.

– Proverbs 20:14

Let nothing be done through strife or vainglory; but in lowliness of mind let each esteem other better than themselves.

– Philippians 2:3

728. Jesus said, "*Be wise as a serpent, and harmless as a dove*". Thus, we should continually be using our keenly refined

senses, to gather the information necessary to safely navigate through the potential dangers in the *jungle of life!*

Behold, I send you forth as sheep in the midst of wolves: be ye therefore wise as serpents, and harmless as doves.

– Matthew 10:16

For when for the time ye ought to be teachers, ye have need that one teach you again which be the first principles of the oracles of God; and are become such as have need of milk, and not of strong meat. For every one that useth milk is unskilful in the word of righteousness: for he is a babe. But strong meat belongeth to them that are of full age, even those who by reason of use have their senses exercised to discern both good and evil.

– Hebrews 5:12–14

729. Faithfulness is a spirit we should all seek to attain and maintain. We must live by faithfulness, and should pass it along to our children, friends, and loved ones. *Hold on* until the end!

Most men will proclaim every one his own goodness: but a faithful man who can find?

– Proverbs 20:6

Now it came to pass, when the wall was built, and I had set up the doors, and the porters and the singers and the Levites were appointed, That I gave my brother Hanani, and

Hananiah the ruler of the palace, charge over Jerusalem: for he was a faithful man, and feared God above many.

— Nehemiah 7:1–2

730. Success is normal. *Failure* is unnatural. You were born to succeed. Failure is what's unnatural.

The blessing of the Lord, it maketh rich, and he addeth no sorrow with it.

— Proverbs 10:22

731. The key to having a happy marriage is to be happy *"one day at a time"*, while you work on being *"happily ever after"*.

Wives, submit yourselves unto your own husbands, as unto the Lord. For the husband is the head of the wife, even as Christ is the head of the church: and he is the saviour of the body. Therefore as the church is subject unto Christ, so let the wives be to their own husbands in every thing. Husbands, love your wives, even as Christ also loved the church, and gave himself for it; That he might sanctify and cleanse it with the washing of water by the word, That he might present it to himself a glorious church, not having spot, or wrinkle, or any such thing; but that it should be holy and without blemish. So ought men to love their wives as their own bodies. He that loveth his wife loveth himself. For no man ever yet hated his own flesh; but nourisheth and cherisheth it, even as the Lord the church: For we are members of his body, of his flesh, and of his bones. For this cause shall a man leave his father and

mother, and shall be joined unto his wife, and they two shall be one flesh. This is a great mystery: but I speak concerning Christ and the church. Nevertheless let every one of you in particular so love his wife even as himself; and the wife see that she reverence her husband.

– Ephesians 5:22–33

732. The quality of your thoughts will determine the quality of your life. You have the power to choose the quality of your thoughts, through choosing the quality of your input. The books, television, movies, music, and people you receive from are shaping your thoughts and perspective of reality.

A good man out of the good treasure of his heart bringeth forth that which is good; and an evil man out of the evil treasure of his heart bringeth forth that which is evil: for of the abundance of the heart his mouth speaketh.

– Luke 6:45

For as he thinketh in his heart, so is he: Eat and drink, saith he to thee; but his heart is not with thee.

– Proverbs 23:7

I will set no wicked thing before mine eyes: I hate the work of them that turn aside; it shall not cleave to me.

– Psalm 101:3

He that walketh with wise men shall be wise: but a companion of fools shall be destroyed.

– Proverbs 13:20

733. The Bible is the Word of God. It is God talking to you and me. We will find comfort, peace, wisdom, and direction from spending time studying it everyday.

Come unto me, all ye that labour and are heavy laden, and I will give you rest. Take my yoke upon you, and learn of me; for I am meek and lowly in heart: and ye shall find rest unto your souls. For my yoke is easy, and my burden is light.

– Matthew 11:28–30

734. God is listening when you pray. God is listening when you praise. He wants to answer you. Call out to Him in prayer. Be faithful in believing. He will answer you. He will come through!

Give ear, O Lord, unto my prayer; and attend to the voice of my supplications. In the day of my trouble I will call upon thee: for thou wilt answer me.

– Psalm 86:6–7

735. You must strengthen yourself on the inside, when you have opposition on the outside.

Gird up thy loins now like a man: I will demand of thee, and declare thou unto me.

– Job 40:7

736. If you spend enough time being truly thankful, you will forget about complaining.

In every thing give thanks: for this is the will of God in Christ Jesus concerning you.

–1 Thessalonians 5:18

737. We must always be looking with our inner eyes, and listening with our inner ears, because there is always more happening on the outside than we can see or hear in the natural.

For though we walk in the flesh, we do not war after the flesh: (For the weapons of our warfare are not carnal, but mighty through God to the pulling down of strong holds;) Casting down imaginations, and every high thing that exalteth itself against the knowledge of God, and bringing into captivity every thought to the obedience of Christ.

–2 Corinthians 10:3–5

Finally, my brethren, be strong in the Lord, and in the power of his might. Put on the whole armour of God, that ye may be able to stand against the wiles of the devil. For we wrestle not against flesh and blood, but against principalities, against powers, against the rulers of the darkness of this world, against spiritual wickedness in high places. Wherefore take unto you the whole armour of God, that ye may be able to withstand in the evil day, and having done all, to stand. Stand therefore, having your loins girt about with truth, and having

on the breastplate of righteousness; And your feet shod with the preparation of the gospel of peace; Above all, taking the shield of faith, wherewith ye shall be able to quench all the fiery darts of the wicked. And take the helmet of salvation, and the sword of the Spirit, which is the word of God: Praying always with all prayer and supplication in the Spirit, and watching thereunto with all perseverance and supplication for all saints.

– Ephesians 6:10–18

738. When you know you've got a *"cake cooling on the stove"*, you don't have to be nervous, cause *"ain't nothing left but the icing!"*

Then said he unto me, Fear not, Daniel: for from the first day that thou didst set thine heart to understand, and to chasten thyself before thy God, thy words were heard, and I am come for thy words.

– Daniel 10:12

And this is the confidence that we have in him, that, if we ask any thing according to his will, he heareth us: and if we know that he hear us, whatsoever we ask, we know that we have the petitions that we desired of him.

–1 John 5:14–15

The Lord is far from the wicked: but he heareth the prayer of the righteous.

– Proverbs 15:29

739. At the end of the day, crass, and crude people never truly succeed. They can have some earthly success for a moment, but only at the expense of compromising their soul and true godly nature.

For what is a man profited, if he shall gain the whole world, and lose his own soul? or what shall a man give in exchange for his soul?

– Matthew 16:26

740. It takes the same measure of faith, hope, and determination in every stage of gaining a harvest. Seed, time, and harvest all require faith, hope, and determination to obtain the harvest.

While the earth remaineth, seedtime and harvest, and cold and heat, and summer and winter, and day and night shall not cease.

– Genesis 8:22

And he said, So is the kingdom of God, as if a man should cast seed into the ground; And should sleep, and rise night and day, and the seed should spring and grow up, he knoweth not how. For the earth bringeth forth fruit of herself; first the blade, then the ear, after that the full corn in the ear. But when the fruit is brought forth, immediately he putteth in the sickle, because the harvest is come.

– Mark 4:26–29

In the morning sow thy seed, and in the evening withhold not thine hand: for thou knowest not whether shall prosper, either this or that, or whether they both shall be alike good.

– Ecclesiastes 11:6

741. Treat everyone like the most important person in the world! It will make you feel better!

Jesus said unto him, Thou shalt love the Lord thy God with all thy heart, and with all thy soul, and with all thy mind. This is the first and great commandment. And the second is like unto it, Thou shalt love thy neighbour as thyself. On these two commandments hang all the law and the prophets.

– Matthew 22:37–40

742. May God deliver you from a "*dead dog*" mentality, and allow you to experience the prosperity, honor, and inheritance of your birthright as a king or queen.

And David said, Is there yet any that is left of the house of Saul, that I may shew him kindness for Jonathan's sake? And there was of the house of Saul a servant whose name was Ziba. And when they had called him unto David, the king said unto him, Art thou Ziba? And he said, Thy servant is he. And the king said, Is there not yet any of the house of Saul, that I may shew the kindness of God unto him? And Ziba said unto the king, Jonathan hath yet a son, which is lame on his feet. And

the king said unto him, Where is he? And Ziba said unto the king, Behold, he is in the house of Machir, the son of Ammiel, in Lodebar. Then king David sent, and fetched him out of the house of Machir, the son of Ammiel, from Lodebar. Now when Mephibosheth, the son of Jonathan, the son of Saul, was come unto David, he fell on his face, and did reverence. And David said, Mephibosheth. And he answered, Behold thy servant! And David said unto him, Fear not: for I will surely shew thee kindness for Jonathan thy father's sake, and will restore thee all the land of Saul thy father; and thou shalt eat bread at my table continually. And he bowed himself, and said, What is thy servant, that thou shouldest look upon such a dead dog as I am? Then the king called to Ziba, Saul's servant, and said unto him, I have given unto thy master's son all that pertained to Saul and to all his house. Thou therefore, and thy sons, and thy servants, shall till the land for him, and thou shalt bring in the fruits, that thy master's son may have food to eat: but Mephibosheth thy master's son shall eat bread alway at my table. Now Ziba had fifteen sons and twenty servants. Then said Ziba unto the king, According to all that my lord the king hath commanded his servant, so shall thy servant do. As for Mephibosheth, said the king, he shall eat at my table, as one of the king's sons. And Mephibosheth had a young son, whose name was Micha. And all that dwelt in the house of Ziba were servants unto Mephibosheth. So Mephibosheth dwelt in Jerusalem: for he did eat continually at the king's table; and was lame on both his feet.

–2 Samuel 9

For to him that is joined to all the living there is hope: for a living dog is better than a dead lion. For the living know that they shall die: but the dead know not any thing, neither have they any more a reward; for the memory of them is forgotten. Also their love, and their hatred, and their envy, is now perished; neither have they any more a portion for ever in any thing that is done under the sun. Go thy way, eat thy bread with joy, and drink thy wine with a merry heart; for God now accepteth thy works. Let thy garments be always white; and let thy head lack no ointment. Live joyfully with the wife whom thou lovest all the days of the life of thy vanity, which he hath given thee under the sun, all the days of thy vanity: for that is thy portion in this life, and in thy labour which thou takest under the sun. Whatsoever thy hand findeth to do, do it with thy might; for there is no work, nor device, nor knowledge, nor wisdom, in the grave, whither thou goest. I returned, and saw under the sun, that the race is not to the swift, nor the battle to the strong, neither yet bread to the wise, nor yet riches to men of understanding, nor yet favour to men of skill; but time and chance happeneth to them all.

– Ecclesiastes 9:4–11

743. If you believe God for a supernatural harvest on the financial seed you have sown in a ministry or church, I recommend that you plant a *natural field or vineyard* to reap natural fruit from.

A man shall be satisfied with good by the fruit of his mouth: and the recompence of a man's hands shall be rendered unto him.

– Proverbs 12:14

744. I *will* do all things through Christ, which strengthens me, because *I can!*

I can do all things through Christ which strengtheneth me.

– Philippians 4:13

745. Did you see Jesus in the message that was preached at your church Sunday? How did He look? How did He sound? Will you recognize Him when He comes? Will you be ready to go back with Him when He returns?

I was in the Spirit on the Lord's day, and heard behind me a great voice, as of a trumpet, Saying, I am Alpha and Omega, the first and the last: and, What thou seest, write in a book, and send it unto the seven churches which are in Asia; unto Ephesus, and unto Smyrna, and unto Pergamos, and unto Thyatira, and unto Sardis, and unto Philadelphia, and unto Laodicea. And I turned to see the voice that spake with me. And being turned, I saw seven golden candlesticks; And in the midst of the seven candlesticks one like unto the Son of man, clothed with a garment down to the foot, and girt about the paps with a golden girdle. His head and his hairs were white like wool, as white as snow; and his eyes were as a flame of fire; And his feet like unto fine brass, as if they burned in a furnace; and his voice as the sound of many waters. And he had in his right hand seven stars: and out of his mouth went a sharp twoedged sword: and his countenance was as the sun shineth in his strength. And when I saw him, I fell at his feet

as dead. And he laid his right hand upon me, saying unto me, Fear not; I am the first and the last: I am he that liveth, and was dead; and, behold, I am alive for evermore, Amen; and have the keys of hell and of death.

– Revelation 1:10–18

746. The foundation for a successful, firm house and life, possess *three* ingredients: wisdom, understanding, and knowledge. The Bible is the first source of wisdom. Studying is the source of understanding. Reading, training, and observation are the source of knowledge.

Through wisdom is an house builded; and by understanding it is established: and by knowledge shall the chambers be filled with all precious and pleasant riches.

– Proverbs 24:3–4

747. There's going to be a little *life* in every life. Some things are a part of being in life. However, you and I have power to affect the outcome of our lives–with God's Word.

There hath no temptation taken you but such as is common to man: but God is faithful, who will not suffer you to be tempted above that ye are able; but will with the temptation also make a way to escape, that ye may be able to bear it.

–1 Corinthians 10:13

A man's belly shall be satisfied with the fruit of his mouth; and with the increase of his lips shall he be filled. Death and life

are in the power of the tongue: and they that love it shall eat the fruit thereof.

– Proverbs 18:20–21

748. Pay for the advice of experts in their field. It will save you a lot of time and *frustration.*

Buy the truth, and sell it not; also wisdom, and instruction, and understanding.

– Proverbs 23:23

Without counsel purposes are disappointed: but in the multitude of counsellors they are established.

– Proverbs 15:22

749. We should be appreciative of every kind word or deed given to us by others, for they truly are life's *unmerited gifts!*

And be ye kind one to another, tenderhearted, forgiving one another, even as God for Christ's sake hath forgiven you.

– Ephesians 4:32

750. You have access to the same Mind that created the universe, and Who calls the hundreds of billions of stars by their names. He is the Alpha and Omega. He is the Ancient of Days! He knows you by your name, and He is well able to give you the wisdom needed for your life. Just ask in fervent prayer and accept it by faith and confidence.

He telleth the number of the stars; he calleth them all by their names. Great is our Lord, and of great power: his understanding is infinite.

– Psalm 147:4–5

And this is the confidence that we have in him, that, if we ask any thing according to his will, he heareth us: and if we know that he hear us, whatsoever we ask, we know that we have the petitions that we desired of him.

–1 John 5:14–15

751. Go ahead and do whatever God has given you to do. It doesn't have to be perfect, for it to be *effective.*

In all labour there is profit: but the talk of the lips tendeth only to penury.

– Proverbs 14:23

752. Here's a key to ongoing success: make a list, work your list, and repeat.

And the Lord answered me, and said, Write the vision, and make it plain upon tables, that he may run that readeth it. For the vision is yet for an appointed time, but at the end it shall speak, and not lie: though it tarry, wait for it; because it will surely come, it will not tarry. Behold, his soul which is lifted up is not upright in him: but the just shall live by his faith.

– Habakkuk 2:2–4

753. The weapons of our warfare don't change. The Devil doesn't change. Only we change in our *consistency* to use the weapons of our warfare.

Finally, my brethren, be strong in the Lord, and in the power of his might. Put on the whole armour of God, that ye may be able to stand against the wiles of the devil. For we wrestle not against flesh and blood, but against principalities, against powers, against the rulers of the darkness of this world, against spiritual wickedness in high places. Wherefore take unto you the whole armour of God, that ye may be able to withstand in the evil day, and having done all, to stand. Stand therefore, having your loins girt about with truth, and having on the breastplate of righteousness; And your feet shod with the preparation of the gospel of peace; Above all, taking the shield of faith, wherewith ye shall be able to quench all the fiery darts of the wicked. And take the helmet of salvation, and the sword of the Spirit, which is the word of God: Praying always with all prayer and supplication in the Spirit, and watching thereunto with all perseverance and supplication for all saints.

– Ephesians 6:10–18

754. Thoughts become *things*, so it's good to *think!*

For as he thinketh in his heart, so is he...

– Proverbs 23:7a

755. Ideas are *money*, so always place the proper *value* on your ideas.

For as he thinketh in his heart, so is he...

– Proverbs 23:7a

The thoughts of the righteous are right...

– Proverbs 12:5a

756. Nothing builds your confidence like *success!*

For I am not ashamed of the gospel of Christ: for it is the power of God unto salvation to every one that believeth; to the Jew first, and also to the Greek. For therein is the righteousness of God revealed from faith to faith: as it is written, The just shall live by faith.

– Romans 1:16–17

757. The more you succeed the more you feel that you *can* succeed.

But we all, with open face beholding as in a glass the glory of the Lord, are changed into the same image from glory to glory, even as by the Spirit of the Lord.

–2 Corinthians 3:18

Distinguished Wisdom Presents . . . "Living Proverbs"–Vol.2

758. May your heart be filled with God's wisdom. May your soul be established in truth. May your mind have full, clear understanding of God's will and ways. And may you have peace. In Jesus name. Amen.

And the spirit of the Lord shall rest upon him, the spirit of wisdom and understanding, the spirit of counsel and might, the spirit of knowledge and of the fear of the Lord; And shall make him of quick understanding in the fear of the Lord: and he shall not judge after the sight of his eyes, neither reprove after the hearing of his ears: But with righteousness shall he judge the poor, and reprove with equity for the meek of the earth: and he shall smite the earth: with the rod of his mouth, and with the breath of his lips shall he slay the wicked. And righteousness shall be the girdle of his loins, and faithfulness the girdle of his reins.

– Isaiah 11:2–5

759. There are many thoughts that may go through your mind about what you had to do today; but what you actually had to do, you *did*. Each day must stand on its on.

Take therefore no thought for the morrow: for the morrow shall take thought for the things of itself. Sufficient unto the day is the evil thereof.

– Matthew 6:34

760. Once you learn *how* to succeed, you can do it over and over again.

The thoughts of the diligent tend only to plenteousness; but of every one that is hasty only to want.

– Proverbs 21:5

761. God has a plan that's greater than man's, and I'm glad to be a *part of it!*

O the depth of the riches both of the wisdom and knowledge of God! How unsearchable are his judgments, and his ways past finding out! For who hath known the mind of the Lord? or who hath been his counsellor? Or who hath first given to him, and it shall be recompensed unto him again? For of him, and through him, and to him, are all things: to whom be glory for ever. Amen.

– Romans 11:33–36

762. The blessing of the Lord makes you abundantly rich! He surrounds you with favor like a shield. And, the joy of the Lord is your strength!

The blessing of the Lord, it maketh rich, and he addeth no sorrow with it.

– Proverbs 10:22

For thou, Lord, wilt bless the righteous; with favour wilt thou compass him as with a shield.

– Psalm 5:12

763. In any endeavor, someone has to have the faith to *keep on dreaming* until the dream comes to pass. If you stop dreaming and working, it won't come to pass.

For a dream cometh through the multitude of business; and a fool's voice is known by multitude of words.

– Ecclesiastes 5:3

764. Sometimes it's not just the *crowd* that you help; sometimes it's the *single person* that makes the grandest difference.

What man of you, having an hundred sheep, if he lose one of them, doth not leave the ninety and nine in the wilderness, and go after that which is lost, until he find it? And when he hath found it, he layeth it on his shoulders, rejoicing. And when he cometh home, he calleth together his friends and neighbours, saying unto them, Rejoice with me; for I have found my sheep which was lost. I say unto you, that likewise joy shall be in heaven over one sinner that repenteth, more than over ninety and nine just persons, which need no repentance. Either what woman having ten pieces of silver, if she lose one piece, doth not light a candle, and sweep the house, and seek diligently till she find it? And when she hath found it, she calleth her friends and her neighbours together, saying, Rejoice with me; for I have found the piece which I had lost. Likewise, I say unto you, there is joy in the presence of the angels of God over one sinner that repenteth.

– Luke 15:4–10

765. You have been *"walking on the water"* this far; there is no need to get nervous now. Just keep on stepping out on the Word of Jesus. He told you to come. You will make it to the other side. You will make it to your promised expected place of blessing!

And straightway Jesus constrained his disciples to get into a ship, and to go before him unto the other side, while he sent the multitudes away. And when he had sent the multitudes away, he went up into a mountain apart to pray: and when the evening was come, he was there alone. But the ship was now in the midst of the sea, tossed with waves: for the wind was contrary. And in the fourth watch of the night Jesus went unto them, walking on the sea. And when the disciples saw him walking on the sea, they were troubled, saying, It is a spirit; and they cried out for fear. But straightway Jesus spake unto them, saying, Be of good cheer; it is I; be not afraid. And Peter answered him and said, Lord, if it be thou, bid me come unto thee on the water. And he said, Come. And when Peter was come down out of the ship, he walked on the water, to go to Jesus. But when he saw the wind boisterous, he was afraid; and beginning to sink, he cried, saying, Lord, save me. And immediately Jesus stretched forth his hand, and caught him, and said unto him, O thou of little faith, wherefore didst thou doubt? And when they were come into the ship, the wind ceased. Then they that were in the ship came and worshipped him, saying, Of a truth thou art the Son of God.

– Matthew 14:22–33

766. You're more than you know. Yet, you're everything that you are, and all that you are will *manifest* soon!

For the earnest expectation of the creature waiteth for the manifestation of the sons of God.

– Romans 8:19

767. The beginning never looks like the end. If you're not able to recognize the beginning of a miracle, you will never see the *fulfillment* of it.

And he said, So is the kingdom of God, as if a man should cast seed into the ground; And should sleep, and rise night and day, and the seed should spring and grow up, he knoweth not how. For the earth bringeth forth fruit of herself; first the blade, then the ear, after that the full corn in the ear. But when the fruit is brought forth, immediately he putteth in the sickle, because the harvest is come.

– Mark 4:26–29

768. Do not allow today's *unbelief*, to cheat you out of tomorrow's *miracle*.

And there were four leprous men at the entering in of the gate: and they said one to another, Why sit we here until we die? If we say, We will enter into the city, then the famine is in the city, and we shall die there: and if we sit still here, we die also. Now therefore come, and let us fall unto the host of the Syrians: if they save us alive, we shall live; and if they kill

us, we shall but die. And they rose up in the twilight, to go unto the camp of the Syrians: and when they were come to the uttermost part of the camp of Syria, behold, there was no man there. For the Lord had made the host of the Syrians to hear a noise of chariots, and a noise of horses, even the noise of a great host: and they said one to another, Lo, the king of Israel hath hired against us the kings of the Hittites, and the kings of the Egyptians, to come upon us. Wherefore they arose and fled in the twilight, and left their tents, and their horses, and their asses, even the camp as it was, and fled for their life. And when these lepers came to the uttermost part of the camp, they went into one tent, and did eat and drink, and carried thence silver, and gold, and raiment, and went and hid it; and came again, and entered into another tent, and carried thence also, and went and hid it. Then they said one to another, We do not well: this day is a day of good tidings, and we hold our peace: if we tarry till the morning light, some mischief will come upon us: now therefore come, that we may go and tell the king's household. So they came and called unto the porter of the city: and they told them, saying, We came to the camp of the Syrians, and, behold, there was no man there, neither voice of man, but horses tied, and asses tied, and the tents as they were. And he called the porters; and they told it to the king's house within. And the king arose in the night, and said unto his servants, I will now shew you what the Syrians have done to us. They know that we be hungry; therefore are they gone out of the camp to hide themselves in the field, saying, When they come out of the city, we shall catch them alive, and get into the city. And one of his servants answered and said, Let some take, I pray thee, five of the horses that remain, which are left in the city, (behold, they

are as all the multitude of Israel that are left in it: behold, I say, they are even as all the multitude of the Israelites that are consumed:) and let us send and see. They took therefore two chariot horses; and the king sent after the host of the Syrians, saying, Go and see. And they went after them unto Jordan: and, lo, all the way was full of garments and vessels, which the Syrians had cast away in their haste. And the messengers returned, and told the king. And the people went out, and spoiled the tents of the Syrians. So a measure of fine flour was sold for a shekel, and two measures of barley for a shekel, according to the word of the Lord. And the king appointed the lord on whose hand he leaned to have the charge of the gate: and the people trode upon him in the gate, and he died, as the man of God had said, who spake when the king came down to him. And it came to pass as the man of God had spoken to the king, saying, Two measures of barley for a shekel, and a measure of fine flour for a shekel, shall be to morrow about this time in the gate of Samaria: And that lord answered the man of God, and said, Now, behold, if the Lord should make windows in heaven, might such a thing be? And he said, Behold, thou shalt see it with thine eyes, but shalt not eat thereof. And so it fell out unto him: for the people trode upon him in the gate, and he died.

–2 Kings 7:3–20

769. How to relate to family, friends, and strangers? Build, strengthen, and encourage–*only*.

From whom the whole body fitly joined together and compacted by that which every joint supplieth, according to

the effectual working in the measure of every part, maketh increase of the body unto the edifying of itself in love.

– Ephesians 4:16

770. You must start with something: because anything can grow to everything it's supposed to be, if you start with *something*.

Now therefore perform the doing of it; that as there was a readiness to will, so there may be a performance also out of that which ye have. For if there be first a willing mind, it is accepted according to that a man hath, and not according to that he hath not.

–2 Corinthians 8:11–12

771. When you *are*, who you are, you will *become* who you are, in spite of who does or doesn't give you *permission* to be who you are. God preordained you.

Then the word of the Lord came unto me, saying, Before I formed thee in the belly I knew thee; and before thou camest forth out of the womb I sanctified thee, and I ordained thee a prophet unto the nations.

– Jeremiah 1:4–5

772. Be sure to maximize your time today. Spend time being productive, by building your business, health, spiritual life, and relationships. Make the most of the day.

So teach us to number our days, that we may apply our hearts unto wisdom.

— Psalm 90:12

773. Sometimes the *"treasures"* we gain from the snow, is just the time we gain to cease from the *"war"* of life, and reflect on the important things of our lives, and to spend time with one another.

Hast thou entered into the treasures of the snow? or hast thou seen the treasures of the hail, which I have reserved against the time of trouble, against the day of battle and war?

— Job 38:22–23

774. Keep making progress in life. To get ahead in *anywise*, is wise.

In all labour there is profit: but the talk of the lips tendeth only to penury.

— Proverbs 14:23

775. I predict a slight spike on the population chart in the next nine months. These are some predictable *"treasures"* in the snow!

Hast thou entered into the treasures of the snow? or hast thou seen the treasures of the hail, which I have reserved against the time of trouble, against the day of battle and war?

– Job 38:22–23

Lo, children are an heritage of the Lord: and the fruit of the womb is his reward.

– Psalm 127:3

776. If you were able to take a hot bath, in a warm home this morning, get food from the fridge, drink clean water, turn on the TV, or look on your cellphone; be thankful for *daily living*: you're blessed more than many!

Blessed be the Lord, who daily loadeth us with benefits, even the God of our salvation. Selah.

– Psalm 68:19

777. Poverty and prosperity are both a state of mind. Whichever you yield to will determine your *reality*.

I beseech you therefore, brethren, by the mercies of God, that ye present your bodies a living sacrifice, holy, acceptable unto God, *which is* your reasonable service. And be not conformed to this world: but be ye transformed by the renewing of your mind, that ye may prove what *is* that good, and acceptable, and perfect, will of God.

– Romans 12:1–2

Beloved, I wish above all things that thou mayest prosper and be in health, even as thy soul prospereth.

–3 John 1:2

778. Faith is a *thinking sport!* It's not just about singing, dancing, and shouting. Faith requires *strategic thinking* in order to be successful in life.

For when for the time ye ought to be teachers, ye have need that one teach you again which be the first principles of the oracles of God; and are become such as have need of milk, and not of strong meat. For every one that useth milk is unskilful in the word of righteousness: for he is a babe. But strong meat belongeth to them that are of full age, even those who by reason of use have their senses exercised to discern both good and evil.

– Hebrews 5:12–14

779. A dream doesn't come to pass by doing only one thing. However, the *multitude* of doing one thing will determine your ultimate success.

For a dream cometh through the multitude of business; and a fool's voice is known by multitude of words.

– Ecclesiastes 5:3

780. When God starts blessing, the Devil starts messing. However, it's up to us to pass the test. *Whose report will you believe?*

Who hath believed our report? and to whom is the arm of the Lord Revealed?

— Isaiah 53:1

The thief cometh not, but for to steal, and to kill, and to destroy: I am come that they might have life, and that they might have it more abundantly.

— John 10:10

Beloved, I wish above all things that thou mayest prosper and be in health, even as thy soul prospereth.

—3 John 1:2

781. When you swim with *"big fish"*, they often splash the size of their dreams over on you!

He that walketh with wise men shall be wise: but a companion of fools shall be destroyed.

— Proverbs 13:20

782. You've got to make some change in order to get some *change* in your *pocket!*

A feast is made for laughter, and wine maketh merry: but money answereth all things.

— Ecclesiastes 10:19

783. Speak what God's Word has said about you. Say, "I am blessed. I am healed. I am rich. I am prosperous. I am righteous. I am redeemed! In Jesus name. Amen."

That he who blesseth himself in the earth shall bless himself in the God of truth; and he that sweareth in the earth shall swear by the God of truth; because the former troubles are forgotten, and because they are hid from mine eyes.

– Isaiah 65:16

784. If you keep on doing the right thing, better and better, learning more and more, you will succeed, and no one can stop you. Your success has already been decreed by God almighty! All you must do is *cooperate* with Him.

Beloved, I wish above all things that thou mayest prosper and be in health, even as thy soul prospereth.

–3 John 1:2

785. I'm always amazed by *unsolicited favor!*

He that diligently seeketh good procureth favour: but he that seeketh mischief, it shall come unto him.

– Proverbs 11:27

786. In regards to being blessed, we have to "*walk by faith and not by sight.*" Yet, often all we have to do is open our eyes

and we will see that we are already in the *middle* of being blessed.

For we walk by faith, not by sight.

–2 Corinthians 5:7

787. Don't worry! God has already blessed you, and there's nothing the Devil can do about it! God has surrounded you with protection, blessing, and favor. He is protecting your family, prospering your job or business, and everything you have on every side. And you are increasing in wealth and wisdom! In Jesus name. Amen!

Hast not thou made an hedge about him, and about his house, and about all that he hath on every side? thou hast blessed the work of his hands, and his substance is increased in the land.

– Job 1:10

788. Don't worry about the future! If you're doing what God has told you to do, all favor is with you! And if God be for you, who can be against you!

And this is the confidence that we have in him, that, if we ask any thing according to his will, he heareth us: and if we know that he hear us, whatsoever we ask, we know that we have the petitions that we desired of him.

–1 John 5:14–15

Now we know that God heareth not sinners: but if any man be a worshipper of God, and doeth his will, him he heareth.

– John 9:31

What shall we then say to these things? If God be for us, who can be against us?

– Romans 8:31

And Jonathan said to the young man that bare his armour, Come, and let us go over unto the garrison of these uncircumcised: it may be that the Lord will work for us: for there is no restraint to the Lord to save by many or by few. And his armourbearer said unto him, Do all that is in thine heart: turn thee; behold, I am with thee according to thy heart.

–1 Samuel 14:6–7

789. Success *"grows on trees!"* Those trees started off as seeds. They were watered and tended for many years. They then eventually bear the fruit of success. Yes, success does grow on trees...if you are willing to go through the process.

But his delight is in the law of the Lord; and in his law doth he meditate day and night. And he shall be like a tree planted by the rivers of water, that bringeth forth his fruit in his season; his leaf also shall not wither; and whatsoever he doeth shall prosper.

– Psalm 1:2–3

790. You can't listen to *small* people, when you have big dreams, because they will instinctively *minimize* your dreams.

And Joseph dreamed a dream, and he told it his brethren: and they hated him yet the more. And he said unto them, Hear, I pray you, this dream which I have dreamed: for, behold, we were binding sheaves in the field, and, lo, my sheaf arose, and also stood upright; and, behold, your sheaves stood round about, and made obeisance to my sheaf. And his brethren said to him, Shalt thou indeed reign over us? or shalt thou indeed have dominion over us? And they hated him yet the more for his dreams, and for his words. And he dreamed yet another dream, and told it his brethren, and said, Behold, I have dreamed a dream more; and, behold, the sun and the moon and the eleven stars made obeisance to me. And he told it to his father, and to his brethren: and his father rebuked him, and said unto him, What is this dream that thou hast dreamed? Shall I and thy mother and thy brethren indeed come to bow down ourselves to thee to the earth? And his brethren envied him; but his father observed the saying.

– Genesis 37:5–11

791. Let's not be like the children of Israel, picking quail out our teeth, burping up manna, with a belly full of water out of the rock, and still complaining! No, let's give thanks in all things for God's abundant blessings!

In every thing give thanks: for this is the will of God in Christ Jesus concerning you.

—1 Thessalonians 5:18

Rejoice in the Lord alway: and again I say, Rejoice.

— Philippians 4:4

Blessed be the Lord, who daily loadeth us with benefits, even the God of our salvation. Selah.

— Psalm 68:19

792. Time advantage is easy to be lost if you don't *maximize* the use of your time.

Boast not thyself of to morrow; for thou knowest not what a day may bring forth.

— Proverbs 27:1

So teach us to number our days, that we may apply our hearts unto wisdom.

— Psalm 90:12

Redeeming the time, because the days are evil.

— Ephesians 5:16

793. Success and distinction in life is a combination of *diligence* and *destiny*. One is our choice and responsibility. The other is God's choice and preordination. However, we have to work together with him for it to come to pass.

But Jesus answered them, My Father worketh hitherto, and I work.

– John 5:17

794. The reason our faith may seem "sometimes up and sometimes down": and it may seem like we "win some and lose some", is because we are *sometimey* in exercising the weapons of our warfare, and principles of God. God's principles *always* work.

For though we walk in the flesh, we do not war after the flesh: (For the weapons of our warfare are not carnal, but mighty through God to the pulling down of strong holds;) Casting down imaginations, and every high thing that exalteth itself against the knowledge of God, and bringing into captivity every thought to the obedience of Christ.

–2 Corinthians 10:3–5

795. There's the ideal and there's the *real*. Let love bridge the gap between the two.

He that covereth a transgression seeketh love; but he that repeateth a matter separateth very friends.

– Proverbs 17:9

796. Great projects, and great work require time to complete. Don't be disappointed if you didn't complete it in one day. Just keep working on it, and you will get it done!

In all labour there is profit: but the talk of the lips tendeth only to penury.

– Proverbs 14:23

797. It's not perfect, it's a process; and if you stay in the process, everything will turn out *fine!*

Brethren, I count not myself to have apprehended: but this one thing I do, forgetting those things which are behind, and reaching forth unto those things which are before, I press toward the mark for the prize of the high calling of God in Christ Jesus.

– Philippians 3:13–14

And we know that all things work together for good to them that love God, to them who are the called according to his purpose. For whom he did foreknow, he also did predestinate to be conformed to the image of his Son, that he might be the firstborn among many brethren.

– Romans 8:28–29

I have fought a good fight, I have finished my course, I have kept the faith: henceforth there is laid up for me a crown of righteousness, which the Lord, the righteous judge, shall give me at that day: and not to me only, but unto all them also that love his appearing.

–2 Timothy 4:7–8

798. We often must say, "*Lord, I believe; help thou my unbelief!*" in obtaining the blessing God has for us. It takes time to build our faith–level to a point that our hearts will *receive* the best God has for us, however through faith we can! Faith comes by hearing the Word!

And straightway the father of the child cried out, and said with tears, Lord, I believe; help thou mine unbelief.

– Mark 9:24

So then faith cometh by hearing, and hearing by the word of God.

– Romans 10:17

799. Don't let an event become the *title* of your story. The name of your story is *victory!* Your life's story is a *universal bestseller!* Many can relate to your challenge. Many can be blessed by your victory. Your test will become your *testimony!*

Looking unto Jesus the author and finisher of our faith; who for the joy that was set before him endured the cross, despising the shame, and is set down at the right hand of the throne of God.

– Hebrews 12:2

800. I have too much peace to *give it away!*

Peace I leave with you, my peace I give unto you: not as the world giveth, give I unto you. Let not your heart be troubled, neither let it be afraid.

– John 14:27

801. Religion may be *regional*, yet truth crosses boundaries.

Jesus saith unto him, I am the way, the truth, and the life: no man cometh unto the Father, but by me.

– John 14:6

802. I'm *too scared* to be broke!

Wisdom is good with an inheritance: and by it there is profit to them that see the sun. For wisdom is a defence, and money is a defence: but the excellency of knowledge is, that wisdom giveth life to them that have it.

– Ecclesiastes 7:11–12

A feast is made for laughter, and wine maketh merry: but money answereth all things.

– Ecclesiastes 10:19

803. The next time that something good happens in your life, simply say, "*That was good! And that was God! And God is good all the time!*"

It is a good thing to give thanks unto the Lord, and to sing praises unto thy name, O Most High: To shew forth thy lovingkindness in the morning, and thy faithfulness every night.

– Psalm 92:1–2

804. A business that you do not invest in will not grow. A *life* that you do not invest in will not grow.

Buy the truth, and sell it not; also wisdom, and instruction, and understanding.

– Proverbs 23:23

805. Listen to good teaching, then make a final judgment. Get wisdom, and then make a decision. The *when, what, how, why* are yours to discern. Those who know the *"way"* may have paved the way before you, but you still have to discern the *timing*.

Buy the truth, and sell it not; also wisdom, and instruction, and understanding.

– Proverbs 23:23

Without counsel purposes are disappointed: but in the multitude of counsellors they are established.

– Proverbs 15:22

806. A little guidance along the way can help you go a *long way!*

Without counsel purposes are disappointed: but in the multitude of counsellors they are established.

– Proverbs 15:22

807. God can relate to you, even when you can't relate to him. He knows you by name. He knows your thoughts afar off. He discerns the intents of your heart, and he always decides in your *favor!*

O Lord, thou hast searched me, and known me. Thou knowest my down sitting and mine uprising, thou understandest my thought afar off. Thou compassest my path and my lying down, and art acquainted with all my ways. For there is not a word in my tongue, but, lo, O Lord, thou knowest it altogether. Thou hast beset me behind and before, and laid thine hand upon me. Such knowledge is too wonderful for me; it is high, I cannot attain unto it. Whither shall I go from thy spirit? or whither shall I flee from thy presence? If I ascend up into heaven, thou art there: if I make my bed in hell, behold, thou art there. If I take the wings of the morning, and dwell in the uttermost parts of the sea; Even there shall thy hand lead me, and thy right hand shall hold me. If I say, Surely the darkness shall cover me; even the night shall be light about me. Yea, the darkness hideth not from thee; but the night shineth as the day: the darkness and the light are both alike to thee. For thou hast possessed my reins: thou hast covered me in my mother's womb. I will praise thee; for I am fearfully and

wonderfully made: marvellous are thy works; and that my soul knoweth right well. My substance was not hid from thee, when I was made in secret, and curiously wrought in the lowest parts of the earth. Thine eyes did see my substance, yet being unperfect; and in thy book all my members were written, which in continuance were fashioned, when as yet there was none of them. How precious also are thy thoughts unto me, O God! how great is the sum of them! If I should count them, they are more in number than the sand: when I awake, I am still with thee. Surely thou wilt slay the wicked, O God: depart from me therefore, ye bloody men. For they speak against thee wickedly, and thine enemies take thy name in vain. Do not I hate them, O Lord, that hate thee? and am not I grieved with those that rise up against thee? I hate them with perfect hatred: I count them mine enemies. Search me, O God, and know my heart: try me, and know my thoughts: And see if there be any wicked way in me, and lead me in the way everlasting.

– Psalm 139

808. Mediocre efforts result into a mediocre life: above average efforts result into an above average life.

Seest thou a man diligent in his business? he shall stand before kings; he shall not stand before mean men.

– Proverbs 22:29

He that diligently seeketh good procureth favour: but he that seeketh mischief, it shall come unto him.

— Proverbs 11:27

For promotion cometh neither from the east, nor from the west, nor from the south. But God is the judge: he putteth down one, and setteth up another.

— Psalm 75:6–7

809. As a saint of God, you must determine what has greater impact in your life, having *"been with Jesus"* or your fears? Choose faith! Choose to be with Jesus!

Now when they saw the boldness of Peter and John, and perceived that they were unlearned and ignorant men, they marvelled; and they took knowledge of them, that they had been with Jesus.

— Acts 4:13

The Lord is on my side; I will not fear: what can man do unto me? The Lord taketh my part with them that help me: therefore shall I see my desire upon them that hate me.

— Psalm 118:6–7

810. In regard to the *"game of life"*: don't get angry get excellent! Many people fight against others, yet, at the end of the day, the most excellent will always *"rise out of the bunch!"* Don't get angry get excellent!

Then this Daniel was preferred above the presidents and princes, because an excellent spirit was in him; and the king

thought to set him over the whole realm. Then the presidents and princes sought to find occasion against Daniel concerning the kingdom; but they could find none occasion nor fault; forasmuch as he was faithful, neither was there any error or fault found in him.

– Daniel 6:3–4

811. In regard to networking: *"the fruit is in the follow–up!"*

He that walketh with wise men shall be wise: but a companion of fools shall be destroyed.

– Proverbs 13:20

The slothful man roasteth not that which he took in hunting: but the substance of a diligent man is precious.

– Proverbs 12:27

812. The benefits of being planted, giving, and growing in a local church, is that you and your family become stronger. You begin to bear lasting fruit. You will remain fruitful and maintain stability, even into older age. You become *proof* of the faithfulness of God.

The righteous shall flourish like the palm tree: he shall grow like a cedar in Lebanon. Those that be planted in the house of the Lord shall flourish in the courts of our God. They shall still bring forth fruit in old age; they shall be fat and flourishing; To shew that the Lord is upright: he is my rock, and there is no unrighteousness in him.

– Psalm 92:12–15

813. In regard to work, the value produced is not always based on the number of hours worked. It is based on the *value* of the activity. Three hours of a higher valued activity, creates greater and more lasting value than 40 hours of a more common activity. Choose your activities *wisely!*

In the morning sow thy seed, and in the evening withhold not thine hand: for thou knowest not whether shall prosper, either this or that, or whether they both shall be alike good.

– Ecclesiastes 11:6

814. The joyful expectation of the righteous shall be gladness. The reward of fulfilling God's steps for living will always be gladness!

The hope of the righteous shall be gladness: but the expectation of the wicked shall perish.

– Proverbs 10:28

815. Never regret sacrificing to do the right thing. It's worth the cost. Never regret giving to help others. God will multiply your seed sown. Be big enough to participate with God, He will always give you back more than you gave Him.

And Amaziah said to the man of God, But what shall we do for the hundred talents which I have given to the army of Israel?

And the man of God answered, The Lord is able to give thee much more than this.

— 2 Chronicles 25:9

816. The key to becoming rich is to think *abundance*, like a rich person. The key to staying rich is to practice *frugality*, like a poor person.

For as he thinketh in his heart, so is he...

— Proverbs 23:7a

He that hath a bountiful eye shall be blessed; for he giveth of his bread to the poor.

— Proverbs 22:9

Be thou diligent to know the state of thy flocks, and look well to thy herds. For riches are not for ever: and doth the crown endure to every generation? The hay appeareth, and the tender grass sheweth itself, and herbs of the mountains are gathered. The lambs are for thy clothing, and the goats are the price of the field. And thou shalt have goats' milk enough for thy food, for the food of thy household, and for the maintenance for thy maidens.

— Proverbs 27:23–27

817. God has great plans for your life. This is the best and most exciting time to be alive. You were born for such a time as this. God has a great plan for you, your children, and your

grandchildren. Live holy and right like He could come tomorrow, but plan and live with positive expectations and make preparations for future generations.

For I know the thoughts that I think toward you, saith the Lord, thoughts of peace, and not of evil, to give you an expected end.

– Jeremiah 29:11

818. The forest is the forest. The jungle is the jungle. *Kings* rule the jungle.

He that walketh with wise men shall be wise: but a companion of fools shall be destroyed.

– Proverbs 13:20

819. We must recognize the difference between a sale and *a seed*.

In the morning sow thy seed, and in the evening withhold not thine hand: for thou knowest not whether shall prosper, either this or that, or whether they both shall be alike good.

– Ecclesiastes 11:6

820. Assume the best, *prepare* for the worst.

The simple believeth every word: but the prudent man looketh well to his going.

– Proverbs 14:15

821. You should get a position. You are young and still excited about life. The money is where life is. If you stay where life is moving, you will move with life. Opportunities will come to those that are a part of the game, whether it is school, church, job, business or each. Stay in life. *You can do it!*

For to him that is joined to all the living there is hope: for a living dog is better than a dead lion. For the living know that they shall die: but the dead know not any thing, neither have they any more a reward; for the memory of them is forgotten. Also their love, and their hatred, and their envy, is now perished; neither have they any more a portion for ever in any thing that is done under the sun. Go thy way, eat thy bread with joy, and drink thy wine with a merry heart; for God now accepteth thy works. Let thy garments be always white; and let thy head lack no ointment. Live joyfully with the wife whom thou lovest all the days of the life of thy vanity, which he hath given thee under the sun, all the days of thy vanity: for that is thy portion in this life, and in thy labour which thou takest under the sun. Whatsoever thy hand findeth to do, do it with thy might; for there is no work, nor device, nor knowledge, nor wisdom, in the grave, whither thou goest. I returned, and saw under the sun, that the race is not to the swift, nor the battle to the strong, neither yet bread to the wise, nor yet riches to men of understanding, nor yet favour to men of skill; but time and chance happeneth to them all.

– Ecclesiastes 9:4–11

822. The world gets smaller, as you get *larger*. It's not as large as you thought it was! We are more connected than you may have thought. As you and I grow, we get closer to even the largest people and places.

For promotion cometh neither from the east, nor from the west, nor from the south. But God is the judge: he putteth down one, and setteth up another.

– Psalm 75:6–7

823. You've got to be *dogged* about making money. You've got to be *tender* about helping people. It takes money to help people.

A feast is made for laughter, and wine maketh merry: but money answereth all things.

– Ecclesiastes 10:19

824. Take time to fulfill what God put you here to do. You are *worth it!* Believe in yourself and what God gave you. If you don't fulfill your dreams, they will go to the grave with you. You will *forfeit* your blessings on the Earth, and your rewards in the Heaven.

Whatsoever thy hand findeth to do, do it with thy might; for there is no work, nor device, nor knowledge, nor wisdom, in the grave, whither thou goest.

– Ecclesiastes 9:10

Wherefore I perceive that there is nothing better, than that a man should rejoice in his own works; for that is his portion: for who shall bring him to see what shall be after him?

— Ecclesiastes 3:22

Every man also to whom God hath given riches and wealth, and hath given him power to eat thereof, and to take his portion, and to rejoice in his labour; this is the gift of God.

— Ecclesiastes 5:19

825. Long-term thinking versus short-term thinking is the difference-maker in success or failure. A lifestyle of participating in church, giving tithes and offerings, bible study, walking in love and forgiveness, diligent smart work, and time management, will create a lifetime result of success, happiness, satisfaction, and reward!

The righteous shall flourish like the palm tree: he shall grow like a cedar in Lebanon. Those that be planted in the house of the Lord shall flourish in the courts of our God. They shall still bring forth fruit in old age; they shall be fat and flourishing; To shew that the Lord is upright: he is my rock, and there is no unrighteousness in him.

— Psalm 92:12–15

826. Our hope is what gives our faith a *reason*.

Now faith is the substance of things hoped for, the evidence of things not seen.

— Hebrews 11:1

827. We were born to rule. We were *born–again* to reign.

And God said, Let us make man in our image, after our likeness: and let them have dominion over the fish of the sea, and over the fowl of the air, and over the cattle, and over all the earth, and over every creeping thing that creepeth upon the earth. So God created man in his own image, in the image of God created he him; male and female created he them. And God blessed them, and God said unto them, Be fruitful, and multiply, and replenish the earth, and subdue it: and have dominion over the fish of the sea, and over the fowl of the air, and over every living thing that moveth upon the earth.

— Genesis 1:26–28

For if by one man's offence death reigned by one; much more they which receive abundance of grace and of the gift of righteousness shall reign in life by one, Jesus Christ.)

— Romans 5:17

828. Deliverance starts *internally*.

I beseech you therefore, brethren, by the mercies of God, that ye present your bodies a living sacrifice, holy, acceptable unto God, which is your reasonable service. And be not conformed to this world: but be ye transformed by the renewing of your mind, that ye may prove what is that good, and acceptable, and perfect, will of God.

– Romans 12:1–2

829. The further the eagle gets away from the nest, the less *significant* the nest becomes.

When I was a child, I spake as a child, I understood as a child, I thought as a child: but when I became a man, I put away childish things.

–1 Corinthians 13:11

830. We should put forth effort to obtain wisdom and knowledge for greater financial increase, for it is the source of getting things done. Yet, all knowledge and wisdom must rest upon a healthy reverence of God, for it is the key to long life, peace, and eternal salvation.

Through wisdom is an house builded; and by understanding it is established: and by knowledge shall the chambers be filled with all precious and pleasant riches.

– Proverbs 24:3–4

The fear of the Lord is the beginning of knowledge: but fools despise wisdom and instruction.

– Proverbs 1:7

A feast is made for laughter, and wine maketh merry: but money answereth all things.

– Ecclesiastes 10:19

For what is a man profited, if he shall gain the whole world, and lose his own soul? or what shall a man give in exchange for his soul?

— Matthew 16:26

831. As a meaningful person, you must continue to fill yourself with meaning! Read, study, listen to, and research meaningful material. It will make your life more *meaningful.*

Buy the truth, and sell it not; also wisdom, and instruction, and understanding.

— Proverbs 23:23

832. There are certain manipulations in society that even a *blind man* would question! However, there is a God who sees all, knows all, and will govern and judge all.

And he cometh to Bethsaida; and they bring a blind man unto him, and besought him to touch him. And he took the blind man by the hand, and led him out of the town; and when he had spit on his eyes, and put his hands upon him, he asked him if he saw ought. And he looked up, and said, I see men as trees, walking. After that he put his hands again upon his eyes, and made him look up: and he was restored, and saw every man clearly.

— Mark 8:22–25

If thou seest the oppression of the poor, and violent perverting of judgment and justice in a province, marvel not

at the matter: for he that is higher than the highest regardeth; and there be higher than they.

– Ecclesiastes 5:8

833. May you and I strive to fulfill God's highest ideals for us today. May we walk in the image that He had when He made us in the beginning. We were made in the image and likeness of God Himself, to reflect His image back to Him from the earth to the heavens.

And God said, Let us make man in our image, after our likeness: and let them have dominion over the fish of the sea, and over the fowl of the air, and over the cattle, and over all the earth, and over every creeping thing that creepeth upon the earth. So God created man in his own image, in the image of God created he him; male and female created he them. And God blessed them, and God said unto them, Be fruitful, and multiply, and replenish the earth, and subdue it: and have dominion over the fish of the sea, and over the fowl of the air, and over every living thing that moveth upon the earth.

– Genesis 1:26–28

I have said, Ye are gods; and all of you are children of the most High.

– Psalm 82:6

834. God doesn't change from day to day in His love towards you. Circumstances may change, and feelings may

change, but be confident that if He was pleased with you yesterday, He is pleased with you today.

Jesus Christ the same yesterday, and to day, and for ever.

– Hebrews 13:8

835. Don't allow anyone to summarize your life into the context of his or her limited frame. The *"author and finisher"* of your life is limitless! And His understanding spans throughout eternity. You are one spirit with Him. You are not *limited!*

But he that is spiritual judgeth all things, yet he himself is judged of no man. For who hath known the mind of the Lord, that he may instruct him? but we have the mind of Christ.

–1 Corinthians 2:15–16

He telleth the number of the stars; he calleth them all by their names. Great is our Lord, and of great power: his understanding is infinite.

– Psalm 147:4–5

836. There is no failure in you! You have a destiny to fulfill! You have already succeeded. God is for you, God is with you, and God is in you! You're destined for success! Failure is not a consideration for you with God on your side. You have a destiny to fulfill! Keep going forward, *full force!*

For we are his workmanship, created in Christ Jesus unto good works, which God hath before ordained that we should walk in them.

– Ephesians 2:10

837. We must take time daily to "*roast*" what we have taken in hunting. We must maximize every opportunity, every gift, every talent, and every resource, to the fullest. What we maximize and appreciate will eventually *feed us!*

The slothful man roasteth not that which he took in hunting: but the substance of a diligent man is precious.

– Proverbs 12:27

838. Don't just be inspired, be principled. Take time daily to become and stay inspired by godly principles, until they become *permanent*. Don't just be inspired be principled.

I beseech you therefore, brethren, by the mercies of God, that ye present your bodies a living sacrifice, holy, acceptable unto God, which is your reasonable service. And be not conformed to this world: but be ye transformed by the renewing of your mind, that ye may prove what is that good, and acceptable, and perfect, will of God.

– Romans 12:1–2

839. The salvation appeal is not about condemnation; it is about an *invitation*.

For God so loved the world, that he gave his only begotten Son, that whosoever believeth in him should not perish, but have everlasting life. For God sent not his Son into the world to condemn the world; but that the world through him might be saved. He that believeth on him is not condemned: but he that believeth not is condemned already, because he hath not believed in the name of the only begotten Son of God. And this is the condemnation, that light is come into the world, and men loved darkness rather than light, because their deeds were evil. For every one that doeth evil hateth the light, neither cometh to the light, lest his deeds should be reproved. But he that doeth truth cometh to the light, that his deeds may be made manifest, that they are wrought in God.

– John 3:16–21

840. A mouth can say anything, but *results* say everything.

For a dream cometh through the multitude of business; and a fool's voice is known by multitude of words.

– Ecclesiastes 5:3

841. Daily love, daily peace, daily joy, daily strength, daily living, daily grace, daily favor, daily wisdom is available to you daily, through daily prayer and daily time in God's Word.

Blessed be the Lord, who daily loadeth us with benefits, even the God of our salvation. Selah.

– Psalm 68:19

842. Don't get trapped into trying to answer hypothetical questions about the future.

–General Colin L. Powell
1996 C–SPAN Interview.

The heart of the righteous studieth to answer: but the mouth of the wicked poureth out evil things.

– Proverbs 15:28

843. In order to finish your course with joy in the accomplishment of great dreams, you have to learn to continually see the glass as *half full*, instead of half empty. You are almost there! Just keep *pouring* into your dreams!

Looking unto Jesus the author and finisher of our faith; who for the joy that was set before him endured the cross, despising the shame, and is set down at the right hand of the throne of God.

– Hebrews 12:2

844. If we do what we need to do, God will do what He has always *desired* to do in our lives.

But whoso looketh into the perfect law of liberty, and continueth therein, he being not a forgetful hearer, but a doer of the work, this man shall be blessed in his deed.

– James 1:25

845. Faith is an "*act*". Act strong, even if you feel weak. Act kind, even if you feel impatient. Act courageous, even if you feel fear. Faith is an *act*. Win a place in *"Faith's Hall of Fame!"* Act in faith, each and every day, and in every situation!

Beat your plowshares into swords and your pruninghooks into spears: let the weak say, I am strong.

— Joel 3:10

Love endures long *and* is patient and kind; love never is envious *nor* boils over with jealousy, is not
boastful *or* vainglorious, does not display itself haughtily.

—1 Corinthians 13:4

Amplified Bible, Classic Edition (AMPC)

Have not I commanded thee? Be strong and of a good courage; be not afraid, neither be thou dismayed: for the Lord thy God is with thee whithersoever thou goest.

— Joshua 1:9

846. Praise God for this new time in your life! This is a time of rejoicing! This is a time of refreshing! This is a time of celebration! It's a time of love. This is your time of new beginnings! Grace and peace be multiplied unto you! In Jesus name. Amen.

And in that day thou shalt say, O Lord, I will praise thee: though thou wast angry with me, thine anger is turned away,

and thou comfortedst me. Behold, God is my salvation; I will trust, and not be afraid: for the Lord Jehovah is my strength and my song; he also is become my salvation. Therefore with joy shall ye draw water out of the wells of salvation. And in that day shall ye say, Praise the Lord, call upon his name, declare his doings among the people, make mention that his name is exalted. Sing unto the Lord; for he hath done excellent things: this is known in all the earth. Cry out and shout, thou inhabitant of Zion: for great is the Holy One of Israel in the midst of thee.

– Isaiah 12

847. On a cloudy day, sing–a–song to make your own sunshine: and smile, to make sunshine for *someone else!*

A merry heart maketh a cheerful countenance: but by sorrow of the heart the spirit is broken.

– Proverbs 15:13

848. God can do *"exceedingly abundantly, above"* all that you could possibly ask or think: but you first have to *think!*

And the Lord said, Behold, the people is one, and they have all one language; and this they begin to do: and now nothing will be restrained from them, which they have imagined to do.

– Genesis 11:6

Now unto him that is able to do exceeding abundantly above all that we ask or think, according to the power that worketh in us.

– Ephesians 3:20

849. View yourself as a diligent person: then, pattern your behavior after what you see inside. Catch a vision of greatness, and you will become greater. You will obtain a position of high status. Your crowd will change from the common and mediocre, to that of greatness, distinction, honor, great influence, and authority.

Seest thou a man diligent in his business? he shall stand before kings; he shall not stand before mean men.

– Proverbs 22:29

850. You only live once, therefore be nice to the people you walk this journey with along the way. We all need the same thing: love, friendship, compassion, and mercy along the way. We all want to be understood, even if you don't have all the answers, your love will make a difference.

And be ye kind one to another, tenderhearted, forgiving one another, even as God for Christ's sake hath forgiven you.

– Ephesians 4:32

851. Decide to be *"full–grown"* today: in thinking, speaking, and understanding. Put away *childish* behavior today. You will increase in favor with God and man.

And Jesus increased in wisdom and stature, and in favour with God and man.

– Luke 2:52

852. Every champion needs a challenge, to stay *relevant*. What's the point of being able to *"leap over a building in a single bound"*, if there's no one to rescue; or to be able to *"run faster than a speeding locomotive"*, if there's nowhere to be. Rise to life's challenges. Be a *champion*!

And what shall I more say? for the time would fail me to tell of Gedeon, and of Barak, and of Samson, and of Jephthae; of David also, and Samuel, and of the prophets: Who through faith subdued kingdoms, wrought righteousness, obtained promises, stopped the mouths of lions. Quenched the violence of fire, escaped the edge of the sword, out of weakness were made strong, waxed valiant in fight, turned to flight the armies of the aliens. Women received their dead raised to life again: and others were tortured, not accepting deliverance; that they might obtain a better resurrection: And others had trial of cruel mockings and scourgings, yea, moreover of bonds and imprisonment: They were stoned, they were sawn asunder, were tempted, were slain with the sword: they wandered about in sheepskins and goatskins; being destitute, afflicted, tormented; (Of whom the world was not worthy:) they wandered in deserts, and in mountains, and in dens and caves

of the earth. And these all, having obtained a good report through faith, received not the promise: God having provided some better thing for us, that they without us should not be made perfect.

– Hebrews 11:32–40

853. A key to *peace during progress* is to know that as long as you keep on moving, you will never be late. When you know you're doing what God said, you can have *peace during progress*

The steps of a good man are ordered by the Lord: and he delighteth in his way. Though he fall, he shall not be utterly cast down: for the Lord upholdeth him with his hand.

– Psalm 37:23–25

854. Learn from the past, but keep your eyes on the *future*. The future is our chief responsibility.

Brethren, I count not myself to have apprehended: but this one thing I do, forgetting those things which are behind, and reaching forth unto those things which are before, I press toward the mark for the prize of the high calling of God in Christ Jesus.

– Philippians 3:13–14

855. *Knowledge* dispels fear. Ignorance is at the root of fear. The more you know and understand about a thing, will

alleviate the fear of the unknown; thus, dispelling the power of fear's grip on your heart, mind, and actions.

My people are destroyed for lack of knowledge: because thou hast rejected knowledge, I will also reject thee, that thou shalt be no priest to me: seeing thou hast forgotten the law of thy God, I will also forget thy children.

– Hosea 4:6

Also, that the soul be without knowledge, it is not good; and he that hasteth with his feet sinneth.

– Proverbs 19:2

856. There is an *"I"* in team. If you don't do your part, and I don't do my part: *"we"* don't win! Therefore, there is an "I" in team. We each have to do our individual part, in order for the team to win; and each should be recognized for their *unique contribution*.

But let every man prove his own work, and then shall he have rejoicing in himself alone, and not in another.

– Galatians 6:4

From whom the whole body fitly joined together and compacted by that which every joint supplieth, according to the effectual working in the measure of every part, maketh increase of the body unto the edifying of itself in love.

– Ephesians 4:16

857. Be thankful for all of the people God has given you to *practice* love upon!

Ye have heard that it hath been said, Thou shalt love thy neighbour, and hate thine enemy. But I say unto you, Love your enemies, bless them that curse you, do good to them that hate you, and pray for them which despitefully use you, and persecute you; That ye may be the children of your Father which is in heaven: for he maketh his sun to rise on the evil and on the good, and sendeth rain on the just and on the unjust. For if ye love them which love you, what reward have ye? do not even the publicans the same? And if ye salute your brethren only, what do ye more than others? do not even the publicans so? Be ye therefore perfect, even as your Father which is in heaven is perfect.

– Matthew 5:43–48

858. Work with a sense of *urgency*, because tomorrow is not promised!

Boast not thyself of to morrow; for thou knowest not what a day may bring forth.

– Proverbs 27:1

859. Your *inputs* determine your *outputs*.

Buy the truth, and sell it not; also wisdom, and instruction, and understanding.

— Proverbs 23:23

860. Everybody's not a *victim*. People eventually *get up*. Then what? Your voice and help, must still be relevant to people who are not desperate. You must provide "*all-temperature cheer!*"

Not for that we have dominion over your faith, but are helpers of your joy: for by faith ye stand.

−2 Corinthians 1:24

861. Results from God, are not about *begging*. It's about obeying. If we obey His principles, the results are measurable, duplicable, and *transferrable* to our children and others.

If they obey and serve him, they shall spend their days in prosperity, and their years in pleasures.

— Job 36:11

862. You are *qualified* to run your own business, you are qualified to be productive, you are qualified to manage your own time, because you are diligent and God *trusts* you.

Go to the ant, thou sluggard; consider her ways, and be wise: which having no guide, overseer, or ruler, provideth her meat in the summer, and gathereth her food in the harvest.

— Proverbs 6:6–8

863. Sometimes *less* words, when rightly spoken can be more effective to the discerning listener, than many words heard by a shallow listener.

The heart of the righteous studieth to answer: but the mouth of the wicked poureth out evil things.

— Proverbs 15:28

The simple believeth every word: but the prudent man looketh well to his going.

— Proverbs 14:15

864. Every step of faith *forward* guarantees success. Every acceptance of complacency guarantees failure. The choice is yours!

The steps of a good man are ordered by the Lord: and he delighteth in his way.

— Psalm 37:23

865. Keep your mind and emotions *flying high!* Don't soar too low, or you will get tangled in the *"trees"* of low expectations, low aspirations, and low performance!

For as he thinketh in his heart, so is he...

— Proverbs 23:7a

866. Progress or the lack thereof, has always been a struggle between creative people with *vision*, and others who lack the creativity to see a vision beyond their current reality.

Where there is no vision, the people perish: but he that keepeth the law, happy is he.

– Proverbs 29:18

867. Keep sowing good seed, because during harvest time, *only* the seed you actually sow will come up!

In the morning sow thy seed, and in the evening withhold not thine hand: for thou knowest not whether shall prosper, either this or that, or whether they both shall be alike good.

– Ecclesiastes 11:6

868. God always plays *fair*. He always abides by His rules. He has certain rules for success in life. We have to play by those rules. If we stay in faith by playing by God's rules, we will get God's rewards. God is no respecter of persons; He is a respecter of faith. If it worked for someone else, it will work for *you!*

But without faith it is impossible to please him: for he that cometh to God must believe that he is, and that he is a rewarder of them that diligently seek him.

– Hebrews 11:6

869. The more you give into life the more life will give into you. People who seize their *"thing"* in life, and really get into their *thing*, the more life will give back to them. The more you give into life, the more life will give into you!

Whatsoever thy hand findeth to do, do it with thy might; for there is no work, nor device, nor knowledge, nor wisdom, in the grave, whither thou goest.

– Ecclesiastes 9:10

870. The tallest buildings, take the longest time to build, and cost the greatest investment of money; yet they yield the highest *revenue streams*, and have the most prestigious and *enduring* reputations.

Therefore whosoever heareth these sayings of mine, and doeth them, I will liken him unto a wise man, which built his house upon a rock: And the rain descended, and the floods came, and the winds blew, and beat upon that house; and it fell not: for it was founded upon a rock. And every one that heareth these sayings of mine, and doeth them not, shall be likened unto a foolish man, which built his house upon the sand: And the rain descended, and the floods came, and the winds blew, and beat upon that house; and it fell: and great was the fall of it.

– Matthew 7:24–27

871. When you have a decision that causes you great consternation, take time to pray. Pray out and find out. Bow

down on your knees. And then when you have peace, follow the direction of the Lord.

Trust in the Lord with all thine heart; and lean not unto thine own understanding. In all thy ways acknowledge him, and he shall direct thy paths.

– Proverbs 3:5–6

872. A nation without morals will become corrupt. Anything that is corrupt will *rot away!* We must choose the right leaders, to restore and preserve the nation.

When the righteous are in authority, the people rejoice: but when the wicked beareth rule, the people mourn.

– Proverbs 29:2

873. *Anytime,* is a good time, to take a *"praise break!"* unto God for all of His goodness, mercy, and lovingkindness to you and your family! Praise Him! It will make you feel better! He deserves it. It's all about Him after all!

It is a good thing to give thanks unto the Lord, and to sing praises unto thy name, O Most High: To shew forth thy lovingkindness in the morning, and thy faithfulness every night.

– Psalm 92:1–2

874. *Fast–Moving* times, require more frequent refueling and revitalization, through constantly spending time seeking God's strength. Take a *"pit–stop"* today to receive God's Word and prayer, so you can make it across the finish line, as an *undeniable victor!*

Seek the Lord and his strength, seek his face continually.

– 1 Chronicles 16:11

875. The Word of God is *"coffee for the soul!"* Take time to sit down with a *"cup"* today. You will be refreshed, revived, and exhilarated by the good news of the Gospel! You deserve a break today! Take time to read the Bible!

Come unto me, all ye that labour and are heavy laden, and I will give you rest. Take my yoke upon you, and learn of me; for I am meek and lowly in heart: and ye shall find rest unto your souls. For my yoke is easy, and my burden is light.

– Matthew 11:28–30

876. A regular Bible reading schedule, creates *order* to your life and thinking. The orderly habit helps to conduct the affairs of your life. Also, be open to *spontaneous* words of revelation as you regularly open the word for encouragement.

And Jesus answered him, saying, It is written, That man shall not live by bread alone, but by every word of God.

– Luke 4:4

877. What do all the angels say on the heavenly team? *"I want to be like Mike!"* Michael is the chief archangel. Jesus is the Head Coach.

But the prince of the kingdom of Persia withstood me one and twenty days: but, lo, Michael, one of the chief princes, came to help me; and I remained there with the kings of Persia.

– Daniel 10:13

878. There is a *"Door to more"*. More joy, more peace, more love, more satisfaction and contentment in life. Jesus is the *Door*. He is the way, the truth, and the life. No one can come back to the Heavenly Father, but by Jesus. He's knocking on the door of your heart. Let Him in, and you will enter into Him.

Behold, I stand at the door, and knock: if any man hear my voice, and open the door, I will come in to him, and will sup with him, and he with me.

– Revelation 3:20

For God so loved the world, that he gave his only begotten Son, that whosoever believeth in him should not perish, but have everlasting life. For God sent not his Son into the world to condemn the world; but that the world through him might be saved. He that believeth on him is not condemned: but he that believeth not is condemned already, because he hath not believed in the name of the only begotten Son of God. And this is the condemnation, that light is come into the world,

and men loved darkness rather than light, because their deeds were evil. For every one that doeth evil hateth the light, neither cometh to the light, lest his deeds should be reproved. But he that doeth truth cometh to the light, that his deeds may be made manifest, that they are wrought in God.

– John 3:16–21

But what saith it? The word is nigh thee, even in thy mouth, and in thy heart: that is, the word of faith, which we preach; that if thou shalt confess with thy mouth the Lord Jesus, and shalt believe in thine heart that God hath raised him from the dead, thou shalt be saved. For with the heart man believeth unto righteousness; and with the mouth confession is made unto salvation. For the scripture saith, Whosoever believeth on him shall not be ashamed. For there is no difference between the Jew and the Greek: for the same Lord over all is rich unto all that call upon him. For whosoever shall call upon the name of the Lord shall be saved.

– Romans 10:8–13

Call out to Him today. Say, "Jesus, Come Into My Heart. I Believe You Are The Son of God. I Believe You Died on The Cross–To Pay For My Sins. I Believe God Raised You From The Dead For My Forgiveness From Sin. I Accept Your Payment For My Sins. I Thank You Now. I Am Forgiven. I Receive Eternal Life. I Am A Christian. I Am Born Again. Thank You. In Jesus Name. Amen."

If you prayed that prayer in sincerity from your heart, you are now a new creature. Your sins are washed away through the

blood of Jesus. Now begin to read the Bible daily. Start reading in the Gospel of John. You will learn more of Who Jesus is. Find a great church in your area that preaches about Jesus and all that God teaches in the Bible. God bless you! You are now born again.

879. Take responsibility to *change the world!* Forgive people before they ask for it, and before they deserve it. This is a way for you to be *proactive* in changing the world. Overcome evil, with good. That's the only way that it will ever change.

Be not overcome of evil, but overcome evil with good.

– Romans 12:21

Ye have heard that it hath been said, Thou shalt love thy neighbour, and hate thine enemy. But I say unto you, Love your enemies, bless them that curse you, do good to them that hate you, and pray for them which despitefully use you, and persecute you; That ye may be the children of your Father which is in heaven: for he maketh his sun to rise on the evil and on the good, and sendeth rain on the just and on the unjust. For if ye love them, which love you, what reward have ye? do not even the publicans the same? And if ye salute your brethren only, what do ye more than others? do not even the publicans so? Be ye therefore perfect, even as your Father, which is in heaven, is perfect.

– Matthew 5:43–48

880. In regards to money and saving, it's not how much you *make*. It's the habits you make and the habits you *break*, that make the difference.

Be thou diligent to know the state of thy flocks, and look well to thy herds. For riches are not for ever: and doth the crown endure to every generation? The hay appeareth, and the tender grass sheweth itself, and herbs of the mountains are gathered. The lambs are for thy clothing, and the goats are the price of the field. And thou shalt have goats' milk enough for thy food, for the food of thy household, and for the maintenance for thy maidens.

– Proverbs 27:23–27

881. Concerning gifts and talents, you must keep the *"wick"* of your passion lit, by taking *extra oil*, so that during the hard times, the downtimes, and the waiting times, your flame will continue to *flare!*

Then shall the kingdom of heaven be likened unto ten virgins, which took their lamps, and went forth to meet the bridegroom. And five of them were wise, and five were foolish. They that were foolish took their lamps, and took no oil with them: But the wise took oil in their vessels with their lamps. While the bridegroom tarried, they all slumbered and slept. And at midnight there was a cry made, Behold, the bridegroom cometh; go ye out to meet him. Then all those virgins arose, and trimmed their lamps. And the foolish said unto the wise, Give us of your oil; for our lamps are gone out. But the wise answered, saying, Not so; lest there be not

enough for us and you: but go ye rather to them that sell, and buy for yourselves. And while they went to buy, the bridegroom came; and they that were ready went in with him to the marriage: and the door was shut. Afterward came also the other virgins, saying, Lord, Lord, open to us. But he answered and said, Verily I say unto you, I know you not. Watch therefore, for ye know neither the day nor the hour wherein the Son of man cometh. For the kingdom of heaven is as a man travelling into a far country, who called his own servants, and delivered unto them his goods. And unto one he gave five talents, to another two, and to another one; to every man according to his several ability; and straightway took his journey. Then he that had received the five talents went and traded with the same, and made them other five talents. And likewise he that had received two, he also gained other two. But he that had received one went and digged in the earth, and hid his lord's money. After a long time the lord of those servants cometh, and reckoneth with them. And so he that had received five talents came and brought other five talents, saying, Lord, thou deliveredst unto me five talents: behold, I have gained beside them five talents more. His lord said unto him, Well done, thou good and faithful servant: thou hast been faithful over a few things, I will make thee ruler over many things: enter thou into the joy of thy lord. He also that had received two talents came and said, Lord, thou deliveredst unto me two talents: behold, I have gained two other talents beside them. His lord said unto him, Well done, good and faithful servant; thou hast been faithful over a few things, I will make thee ruler over many things: enter thou into the joy of thy lord. Then he which had received the one talent came and said, Lord, I knew thee that thou art an hard

man, reaping where thou hast not sown, and gathering where thou hast not strawed: And I was afraid, and went and hid thy talent in the earth: lo, there thou hast that is thine. His lord answered and said unto him, Thou wicked and slothful servant, thou knewest that I reap where I sowed not, and gather where I have not strawed: Thou oughtest therefore to have put my money to the exchangers, and then at my coming I should have received mine own with usury. Take therefore the talent from him, and give it unto him, which hath ten talents. For unto every one that hath shall be given, and he shall have abundance: but from him that hath not shall be taken away even that which he hath.

– Matthew 25:1–29

882. What seemed like a dream will soon prove true. Through faith there's nothing that you and God can't do. Put your trust in God's Word. Put your hands to the plow. And what seemed like a dream will prove true, *now!*

For a dream cometh through the multitude of business; and a fool's voice is known by multitude of words.

– Ecclesiastes 5:3

883. There is no lower class, or upper class, or middle class. We were all created in *God's class!* What determines where you are in life, is what you *learned* in the *"class of life"*. If you learned good, sound financial and life principles, and hearkened to them, you will be elevated in life.

I have said, Ye are gods; and all of you are children of the most High.

– Psalm 82:6

The ransom of a man's life are his riches: but the poor heareth not rebuke.

– Proverbs 13:8

884. Poor people exalt the car, over the house. Rich people exalt the house, over the car. Wealthy people exalt the *land*, over the house.

I love them that love me; and those that seek me early shall find me. Riches and honour are with me; yea, durable riches and righteousness. My fruit is better than gold, yea, than fine gold; and my revenue than choice silver. I lead in the way of righteousness, in the midst of the paths of judgment: That I may cause those that love me to inherit substance; and I will fill their treasures.

– Proverbs 8:17–21

885. There is nothing as humbling as sincere thankfulness. It takes humility to be sincerely thankful.

And it came to pass, as he went to Jerusalem, that he passed through the midst of Samaria and Galilee. And as he entered into a certain village, there met him ten men that were lepers, which stood afar off: And they lifted up their voices, and said, Jesus, Master, have mercy on us. And when he saw them, he

said unto them, Go shew yourselves unto the priests. And it came to pass, that, as they went, they were cleansed. And one of them, when he saw that he was healed, turned back, and with a loud voice glorified God, And fell down on his face at his feet, giving him thanks: and he was a Samaritan. And Jesus answering said, Were there not ten cleansed? But where are the nine? There are not found that returned to give glory to God, save this stranger. And he said unto him, Arise, go thy way: thy faith hath made thee whole.

–Luke 17:11–19

886. Everyone is living in a body. Everyone has to do the best they can with what they have. We have to seek to extend our happiness and joy, as far as we can take it. Invest in your spiritual, mental, physical, social, and financial peace: and live long, strong, and vibrant.

So teach us to number our days, that we may apply our hearts unto wisdom.

– Psalm 90:12

887. Shoot for the *moon!* For you won't be the first person to have gotten there! It's been done before, and you can do it too! There's nothing impossible to them that believe!

I can do all things through Christ which strengtheneth me.

– Philippians 4:13

For with God nothing shall be impossible.

– Luke 1:37

888. You can always improve something that is. You can't improve something that *ain't!*

In the morning sow thy seed, and in the evening withhold not thine hand: for thou knowest not whether shall prosper, either this or that, or whether they both shall be alike good.

– Ecclesiastes 11:6

889. God's laws are the *bones* of the body: strong, stable, and unyielding. God's grace is the *flesh*, sensitive and informing. The Holy Spirit is the *blood* flowing through, delivering life-giving nutrition to the parts. Build your life in God's Word, the Bible. You will flourish, thrive, and be a part of the everlasting Body of Christ.

I am the true vine, and my Father is the husbandman. Every branch in me that beareth not fruit he taketh away: and every branch that beareth fruit, he purgeth it, that it may bring forth more fruit. Now ye are clean through the word, which I have spoken unto you.

– John 15:1–3

890. The way to settle ambiguity is to make a *decision*.

Multitudes, multitudes in the valley of decision: for the day of the Lord is near in the valley of decision.

— Joel 3:14

891. The question is the *answer*. There are certain questions we ask, that are the answer, by virtue of us having to even ask the question.

To do justice and judgment is more acceptable to the Lord than sacrifice.

— Proverbs 21:3

892. Today is another opportunity to *"get it right!"* It is an opportunity to make that change. It is an opportunity to start saving money, eating right, exercising, forgive others, forgive yourself, change your attitude, manage your time, start that business, etc. This is the day that the Lord has made. This is the day of your salvation!

This is the Lord's doing; it is marvellous in our eyes. This is the day, which the Lord hath made; we will rejoice and be glad in it. Save now, I beseech thee, O Lord: O Lord, I beseech thee, send now prosperity.

— Psalm 118:23–25

893. At the end of the day, when all the struggling, strife, and pride is done; after we've attempted to *outdo* the next person; after we've won all the *"marbles in the pile"*...we won't have anything permanent, if we haven't pleased God, through an obedient relationship with the Lord Jesus Christ.

For to him that is joined to all the living there is hope: for a living dog is better than a dead lion. For the living know that they shall die: but the dead know not any thing, neither have they any more a reward; for the memory of them is forgotten. Also their love, and their hatred, and their envy, is now perished; neither have they any more a portion for ever in any thing that is done under the sun. Go thy way, eat thy bread with joy, and drink thy wine with a merry heart; for God now accepteth thy works. Let thy garments be always white; and let thy head lack no ointment. Live joyfully with the wife whom thou lovest all the days of the life of thy vanity, which he hath given thee under the sun, all the days of thy vanity: for that is thy portion in this life, and in thy labour which thou takest under the sun. Whatsoever thy hand findeth to do, do it with thy might; for there is no work, nor device, nor knowledge, nor wisdom, in the grave, whither thou goest.

– Ecclesiastes 9:4–10

894. You must do a lot of work "*above–the–line*", before it positively impacts the bottom–line.

In the morning sow thy seed, and in the evening withhold not thine hand: for thou knowest not whether shall prosper, either this or that, or whether they both shall be alike good.

– Ecclesiastes 11:6

895. Influence without *money*: is like power without *authority*. You may be able to move the pieces on the board, yet at the end of the day someone else *owns the game*.

Also, that the soul be without knowledge, it is not good; and he that hasteth with his feet sinneth.

– Proverbs 19:2

896. Messages of *inability* won't help you be all you can be. You need someone to help inspire the fire of *possibility*, in order for you to believe that you can be and do what you were destined to be and do. Even a child's natural tendency is to say, *"I can do it...!"*

I can do all things through Christ, which strengtheneth me.

– Philippians 4:13

897. Each person has the *responsibility* to be successful. God expects us to be successful. If we fail to take on that responsibility, we fail God. And we waste the space of grace God has given us to taste the *"grapes of success"* in this good land of plenty for all!

And they came unto the brook of Eshcol, and cut down from thence a branch with one cluster of grapes, and they bare it between two upon a staff; and they brought of the pomegranates, and of the figs. The place was called the brook Eshcol, because of the cluster of grapes, which the children of Israel cut down from thence. And they returned from searching of the land after forty days. And they went and came to Moses, and to Aaron, and to all the congregation of the children of Israel, unto the wilderness of Paran, to Kadesh; and brought back word unto them, and unto all the

congregation, and shewed them the fruit of the land. And they told him, and said, We came unto the land whither thou sentest us, and surely it floweth with milk and honey; and this is the fruit of it. Nevertheless the people be strong that dwell in the land, and the cities are walled, and very great: and moreover we saw the children of Anak there. The Amalekites dwell in the land of the south: and the Hittites, and the Jebusites, and the Amorites, dwell in the mountains: and the Canaanites dwell by the sea, and by the coast of Jordan. And Caleb stilled the people before Moses, and said, Let us go up at once, and possess it; for we are well able to overcome it. But the men that went up with him said, We be not able to go up against the people; for they are stronger than we. And they brought up an evil report of the land which they had searched unto the children of Israel, saying, The land, through which we have gone to search it, is a land that eateth up the inhabitants thereof; and all the people that we saw in it are men of a great stature. And there we saw the giants, the sons of Anak, which come of the giants: and we were in our own sight as grasshoppers, and so we were in their sight.

— Numbers 13:23–33

898. Fear, anger, and manipulation are unhealthy bases for relationships. All friendships, relationships, business alliances, and associations should be based on willing freedom and mutual respect.

Now the Lord is that Spirit: and where the Spirit of the Lord is, there is liberty.

–2 Corinthians 3:17

There is no fear in love; but perfect love casteth out fear: because fear hath torment. He that feareth is not made perfect in love.

–1 John 4:18

899. Go ahead and succeed! There are more for you, than could possibly be against you. Even your enemies will stand at peace with you, if you go ahead and succeed to serve all mankind. God is for you. Your family is for you. The government is for you. Society is for you. The heaven and earth is for you, if you will serve the world. Who else makes a *difference?*

What shall we then say to these things? If God be for us, who can be against us?

– Romans 8:31

When a man's ways please the Lord, he maketh even his enemies to be at peace with him.

– Proverbs 16:7

Be strong and courageous, be not afraid nor dismayed for the king of Assyria, nor for all the multitude that is with him: for there be more with us than with him: with him is an arm of flesh; but with us is the Lord our God to help us, and to fight our battles. And the people rested themselves upon the words of Hezekiah king of Judah.

–2 Chronicles 32:7–8

900. Our body is the temple for the Holy Ghost. If we actively and intentionally destroy *God's property*, He will let us! You will get just what you are asking for, because you are sovereign in your decision to live or die. The invitation for life is presented to you, however. Only you can choose!

I call heaven and earth to record this day against you, that I have set before you life and death, blessing and cursing: therefore choose life, that both thou and thy seed may live.

– Deuteronomy 30:19

901. It takes *something*, to do something. Success is not for the faint of heart!

If thou faint in the day of adversity, thy strength is small.

– Proverbs 24:10

902. Don't believe for some form of *quasi–success*. For when you truly succeed you'll be known for it. It will be evident to all. It will be *"durable riches"* that will last from generation to generation. It will be stable, and people will clearly see it.

The crown of the wise is their riches: but the foolishness of fools is folly.

– Proverbs 14:24

903. It's much simpler to manage the *truth* about yourself and what you do, than to manage how others *perceive* you. Your truth will speak much louder than the perception you try to manage or navigate or manipulate. Truth speaks louder than anything else.

He that is despised, and hath a servant, is better than he that honoureth himself, and lacketh bread.

– Proverbs 12:9

904. When you have *something*, you have something to improve. When you have nothing, you have nothing to improve. Improvement starts with *something*.

Now therefore perform the doing of it; that as there was a readiness to will, so there may be a performance also out of that which ye have. For if there be first a willing mind, it is accepted according to that a man hath, and not according to that he hath not.

–2 Corinthians 8:11–12

905. Believe God for a long life, full of robust health, energy, and strength. Don't plan to leave here too early. God is able to sustain your health for years. In obeying His Word, is *life more abundantly!*

And the Lord said, My spirit shall not always strive with man, for that he also is flesh: yet his days shall be an hundred and twenty years.

– Genesis 6:3

906. In spite of our human frailties, may we make kindness, courtesy, and consideration the *hallmarks* of our lives as we interact with one another.

And be ye kind one to another, tenderhearted, forgiving one another, even as God for Christ's sake hath forgiven you.

– Ephesians 4:32

907. Unnecessary trouble is *unnecessary*. Necessary trouble is *necessary*. Avoid the one, embrace the other, and handle your business.

Brethren, be not children in understanding: howbeit in malice be ye children, but in understanding be men.

–1 Corinthians 14:20

908. There's nothing as frustrating as the tension of a retracted arrow targeted toward a great outcome. There's nothing as rewarding as an arrow that *launches* and hits the "bull's–eye" for which it was targeted.

Hope deferred maketh the heart sick: but *when* the desire cometh, *it is* a tree of life.

– Proverbs 13:12

909. The tension of a certain amount of resistance makes the pleasure of accomplishment even greater when the *reward* comes!

Hope deferred maketh the heart sick: but *when* the desire cometh, *it is* a tree of life.

– Proverbs 13:12

910. Everything takes time, but money is an *accelerator*. Therefore, we should work as fast as possible to get as much money as we can to accelerate our dreams! Because time is running out!

Whatsoever thy hand findeth to do, do it with thy might; for there is no work, nor device, nor knowledge, nor wisdom, in the grave, whither thou goest.

– Ecclesiastes 9:10

911. If you are a perfectionist, the goal of perfection may not be possible. Yet, you should at least get it to the point, that a *non–perfectionist* could not tell the difference.

Brethren, I count not myself to have apprehended: but this one thing I do, forgetting those things which are behind, and reaching forth unto those things which are before, I press toward the mark for the prize of the high calling of God in Christ Jesus.

– Philippians 3:13–14

912. Find your *place*, for in that space, you will find your taste of sovereignty.

And God said, Let us make man in our image, after our likeness: and let them have dominion over the fish of the sea, and over the fowl of the air, and over the cattle, and over all the earth, and over every creeping thing that creepeth upon the earth. So God created man in his own image, in the image of God created he him; male and female created he them. And God blessed them, and God said unto them, Be fruitful, and multiply, and replenish the earth, and subdue it: and have dominion over the fish of the sea, and over the fowl of the air, and over every living thing that moveth upon the earth.

– Genesis 1:26–28

I have said, Ye are gods; and all of you are children of the most High.

– Psalm 82:6

The ransom of a man's life are his riches: but the poor heareth not rebuke.

– Proverbs 13:8

913. Don't allow your faith to be *infected* by negative, disappointed people, who refuse to take life's medicine of success. Rather, vaccinate your spirit, by soaring higher through enjoying the revitalizing medicine that comes from the joy of achievement!

The desire accomplished is sweet to the soul: but it is abomination to fools to depart from evil.

– Proverbs 13:19

914. People who refuse correction end up poor, in prison, or dead before their time.

The ransom of a man's life are his riches: but the poor heareth not rebuke.

– Proverbs 13:8

915. Don't allow mediocre endeavors, to cheat you out of *exceptional achievements.*

He that tilleth his land shall be satisfied with bread: but he that followeth vain persons is void of understanding.

– Proverbs 12:11

So teach us to number our days, that we may apply our hearts unto wisdom.

– Psalm 90:12

Much food is in the tillage of the poor: but there is that is destroyed for want of judgment.

– Proverbs 13:23

He that walketh with wise men shall be wise: but a companion of fools shall be destroyed.

– Proverbs 13:20

916. We all have the same amount of time every week with 168 hours. Some waste it, by engaging in *inferior* endeavors. Some maximize it, to create enduring value. Yet, even an *"ant"* can build themselves a suitable home with the *"sands of time"* that we waste each day!

Go to the ant, thou sluggard; consider her ways, and be wise: which having no guide, overseer, or ruler, provideth her meat in the summer, and gathereth her food in the harvest.

– Proverbs 6:6–8

917. The world is not going down on my *watch*, because I have too much to do! It will end; yet, I have to do my part first. If I'm wrong, I will go to heaven and receive my eternal reward, because when Jesus comes, he will find me *"occupying"* until he comes.

He said therefore, A certain nobleman went into a far country to receive for himself a kingdom, and to return. And he called his ten servants, and delivered them ten pounds, and said unto them, Occupy till I come.

– Luke 19:12–13

918. Our hope is what gives our faith, *a reason*. We must hope for something greater, in order to be stimulated to pursue something greater. Our hope is what gives our faith a reason.

For a dream cometh through the multitude of business; and a fool's voice is known by multitude of words.

– Ecclesiastes 5:3

919. The more you give into life the more *life* gives into you.

There is that scattereth, and yet increaseth; and there is that withholdeth more than is meet, but it tendeth to poverty. The liberal soul shall be made fat: and he that watereth shall be watered also himself.

– Proverbs 11:24–25

920. Jesus came to the earth, to die in our place on the cross– to pay for our sins. God the Father forgave all of our sins, through the sacrifice of Jesus. The Father raised Jesus from the dead, after he spent three days in the grave; so you and I can now have eternal life in heaven, and life more abundantly on earth!

The thief cometh not, but for to steal, and to kill, and to destroy: I am come that they might have life, and that they might have it more abundantly.

– John 10:10

921. My message is not just about confessing. It's about *possessing!* Let us go up at once, for we are well able to possess the land!

And they told him, and said, We came unto the land whither thou sentest us, and surely it floweth with milk and honey; and this is the fruit of it. Nevertheless the people be strong that dwell in the land, and the cities are walled, and very great: and moreover we saw the children of Anak there. The Amalekites dwell in the land of the south: and the Hittites, and the Jebusites, and the Amorites, dwell in the mountains: and the Canaanites dwell by the sea, and by the coast of Jordan. And Caleb stilled the people before Moses, and said, Let us go up at once, and possess it; for we are well able to overcome it.

– Numbers 13:27–30

922. Succeeding with God is like driving a car. God provides the vehicle, the motor, and the gas; yet, you must put your foot on the *accelerator*. You must fill–up with the fuel of joy, to stay full of motivation. You must work with God to succeed. Yet, he has already provided the vehicle, the tools, and the destination!

For we are his workmanship, created in Christ Jesus unto good works, which God hath before ordained that we should walk in them.

– Ephesians 2:10

923. I am human, and I am healed. I am *human*, in that, I am touched with the same infirmities that anyone can be touched with. I am *healed*, because of the resurrection power of the

Lord Jesus Christ. I am human, and I am healed, because of the blood of Jesus Christ!

But he was wounded for our transgressions, he was bruised for our iniquities: the chastisement of our peace was upon him; and with his stripes we are healed.

– Isaiah 53:5

924. We should learn to utilize all the technology, knowledge, science, and skill that God has made available for us to live and have *dominion* in the earth. And at the end of the day we must always recognize that He is sovereign and in ultimate control.

The heaven, even the heavens, are the Lord's: but the earth hath he given to the children of men.

– Psalm 115:16

925. Don't get upset. Get it done. Don't be offended. Be effective.

This twenty years have I been with thee; thy ewes and thy she goats have not cast their young, and the rams of thy flock have I not eaten. That which was torn of beasts I brought not unto thee; I bare the loss of it; of my hand didst thou require it, whether stolen by day, or stolen by night. Thus I was; in the day the drought consumed me, and the frost by night; and my sleep departed from mine eyes. Thus have I been twenty years in thy house; I served thee fourteen years for thy two daughters, and six years for thy cattle: and thou hast changed

my wages ten times. Except the God of my father, the God of Abraham, and the fear of Isaac, had been with me, surely thou hadst sent me away now empty. God hath seen mine affliction and the labour of my hands, and rebuked thee yesternight.

– Genesis 31:38–42

926. Run as *fast* as you can to fulfill God's plan for your life. You are not in competition with anyone else. Just win *your* race, and you will be a champion in your *own* life's race.

I have fought a good fight, I have finished my course, I have kept the faith: henceforth there is laid up for me a crown of righteousness, which the Lord, the righteous judge, shall give me at that day: and not to me only, but unto all them also that love his appearing.

–2 Timothy 4:7–8

927. In the midst of what seems to be your darkest hour, when it seems that no one else is dependable; God will strengthen you to do your most important deed. You were made for something great. You have entered the world for a purpose. Submit to God, by accepting Jesus Christ, God's only begotten Son. You will accomplish your purpose! You will overcome your greatest enemies: *sin, death, and hell!*

For God so loved the world, that he gave his only begotten Son, that whosoever believeth in him should not perish, but have everlasting life. For God sent not his Son into the world to condemn the world; but that the world through him might

be saved. He that believeth on him is not condemned: but he that believeth not is condemned already, because he hath not believed in the name of the only begotten Son of God. And this is the condemnation, that light is come into the world, and men loved darkness rather than light, because their deeds were evil. For every one that doeth evil hateth the light, neither cometh to the light, lest his deeds should be reproved. But he that doeth truth cometh to the light, that his deeds may be made manifest, that they are wrought in God.

– John 3:16–21

928. When the blessings start coming down, don't get too busy to keep the *praises* rising up! Just like rain evaporating into the clouds, you must keep your clouds of blessings full of praises, in order for them to continue to shower blessings down upon your life!

Blessed be the Lord, who daily loadeth us with benefits, even the God of our salvation. Selah.

– Psalm 68:19

It is a good thing to give thanks unto the Lord, and to sing praises unto thy name, O Most High: To shew forth thy lovingkindness in the morning, and thy faithfulness every night.

– Psalm 92:1–2

929. As a leader, just keep loving and leading. Don't be distracted by *emotions*. Don't be turned around because of doubts. Just keep stepping, praying, loving, and leading.

And when Pharaoh drew nigh, the children of Israel lifted up their eyes, and, behold, the Egyptians marched after them; and they were sore afraid: and the children of Israel cried out unto the Lord. And they said unto Moses, Because there were no graves in Egypt, hast thou taken us away to die in the wilderness? Wherefore hast thou dealt thus with us, to carry us forth out of Egypt? Is not this the word that we did tell thee in Egypt, saying, Let us alone, that we may serve the Egyptians? For it had been better for us to serve the Egyptians, than that we should die in the wilderness. And Moses said unto the people, Fear ye not, stand still, and see the salvation of the Lord, which he will shew to you to day: for the Egyptians whom ye have seen to day, ye shall see them again no more for ever. The Lord shall fight for you, and ye shall hold your peace. And the Lord said unto Moses, Wherefore criest thou unto me? Speak unto the children of Israel, that they go forward: But lift thou up thy rod, and stretch out thine hand over the sea, and divide it: and the children of Israel shall go on dry ground through the midst of sea. And I, behold, I will harden the hearts of the Egyptians, and they shall follow them: and I will get me honour upon Pharaoh, and upon all his host, upon his chariots, and upon his horsemen. And the Egyptians shall know that I am the Lord, when I have gotten me honour upon Pharaoh, upon his chariots, and upon his horsemen. And the angel of God, which went before the camp of Israel, removed and went behind

them; and the pillar of the cloud went from before their face, and stood behind them: And it came between the camp of the Egyptians and the camp of Israel; and it was a cloud and darkness to them, but it gave light by night to these: so that the one came not near the other all the night. And Moses stretched out his hand over the sea; and the Lord caused the sea to go back by a strong east wind all that night, and made the sea dry land, and the waters were divided. And the children of Israel went into the midst of the sea upon the dry ground: and the waters were a wall unto them on their right hand, and on their left. And it came to pass, that in the morning watch the Lord looked unto the host of the Egyptians through the pillar of fire and of the cloud, and troubled the host of the Egyptians, And took off their chariot wheels, that they drave them heavily: so that the Egyptians said, Let us flee from the face of Israel; for the Lord fighteth for them against the Egyptians. And Moses stretched forth his hand over the sea, and the sea returned to his strength when the morning appeared; and the Egyptians fled against it; and the Lord overthrew the Egyptians in the midst of the sea. And the waters returned, and covered the chariots, and the horsemen, and all the host of Pharaoh that came into the sea after them; there remained not so much as one of them. But the children of Israel walked upon dry land in the midst of the sea; and the waters were a wall unto them on their right hand, and on their left. Thus the Lord saved Israel that day out of the hand of the Egyptians; and Israel saw the Egyptians dead upon the sea shore.

–Exodus 14:10–30

930. May you be expanded to your full *capacity*. May you be totally filled with God, so that you take the full shape of who you were created to be! In Jesus name. Amen.

And God said, Let us make man in our image, after our likeness: and let them have dominion over the fish of the sea, and over the fowl of the air, and over the cattle, and over all the earth, and over every creeping thing that creepeth upon the earth. So God created man in his own image, in the image of God created he him; male and female created he them. And God blessed them, and God said unto them, Be fruitful, and multiply, and replenish the earth, and subdue it: and have dominion over the fish of the sea, and over the fowl of the air, and over every living thing that moveth upon the earth.

– Genesis 1:26–28

I have said, Ye are gods; and all of you are children of the most High.

– Psalm 82:6

And ye are complete in him, which is the head of all principality and power.

– Colossians 2:10

And to know the love of Christ, which passeth knowledge, that ye might be filled with all the fulness of God.

– Ephesians 3:19

931. The highest service is *success*. You can't help anyone else, if you can't help yourself. The highest service is success.

A feast is made for laughter, and wine maketh merry: but money answereth all things.

– Ecclesiastes 10:19

932. In regards to marriage, anticipation is the key to happiness. Being able to *anticipate* the needs and desires of your spouse is the key to happiness.

Likewise, ye husbands, dwell with them according to knowledge, giving honour unto the wife, as unto the weaker vessel, and as being heirs together of the grace of life; that your prayers be not hindered. Finally, be ye all of one mind, having compassion one of another, love as brethren, be pitiful, be courteous.

–1 Peter 3:7–8

933. God knows how to turn a *destiny* story out of a difficult story. Even when things don't make sense in the beginning, God can turn it into a happy destiny ending!

And Joseph dreamed a dream, and he told it his brethren: and they hated him yet the more. And he said unto them, Hear, I pray you, this dream which I have dreamed: for, behold, we were binding sheaves in the field, and, lo, my sheaf arose, and also stood upright; and, behold, your sheaves stood round about, and made obeisance to my sheaf. And his brethren said

to him, Shalt thou indeed reign over us? or shalt thou indeed have dominion over us? And they hated him yet the more for his dreams, and for his words. And he dreamed yet another dream, and told it his brethren, and said, Behold, I have dreamed a dream more; and, behold, the sun and the moon and the eleven stars made obeisance to me. And he told it to his father, and to his brethren: and his father rebuked him, and said unto him, What is this dream that thou hast dreamed? Shall I and thy mother and thy brethren indeed come to bow down ourselves to thee to the earth? And his brethren envied him; but his father observed the saying.

– Genesis 37:5–11

And when they saw him afar off, even before he came near unto them, they conspired against him to slay him. And they said one to another, Behold, this dreamer cometh. Come now therefore, and let us slay him, and cast him into some pit, and we will say, Some evil beast hath devoured him: and we shall see what will become of his dreams.

– Genesis 37:18–20

And the sons of Israel came to buy corn among those that came: for the famine was in the land of Canaan. And Joseph was the governor over the land, and he it was that sold to all the people of the land: and Joseph's brethren came, and bowed down themselves before him with their faces to the earth. And Joseph saw his brethren, and he knew them, but made himself strange unto them, and spake roughly unto them; and he said unto them, Whence come ye? And they said, From the land of Canaan to buy food. And Joseph knew

his brethren, but they knew not him. And Joseph remembered the dreams, which he dreamed of them, and said unto them, Ye are spies; to see the nakedness of the land ye are come. And they said unto him, Nay, my lord, but to buy food are thy servants come.

– Genesis 42:5–10

Now therefore be not grieved, nor angry with yourselves, that ye sold me hither: for God did send me before you to preserve life. For these two years hath the famine been in the land: and yet there are five years, in the which there shall neither be earing nor harvest. And God sent me before you to preserve you a posterity in the earth, and to save your lives by a great deliverance. So now it was not you that sent me hither, but God: and he hath made me a father to Pharaoh, and lord of all his house, and a ruler throughout all the land of Egypt. Haste ye, and go up to my father, and say unto him, Thus saith thy son Joseph, God hath made me lord of all Egypt: come down unto me, tarry not: and thou shalt dwell in the land of Goshen, and thou shalt be near unto me, thou, and thy children, and thy children's children, and thy flocks, and thy herds, and all that thou hast: and there will I nourish thee; for yet there are five years of famine; lest thou, and thy household, and all that thou hast, come to poverty.

– Genesis 45:5–11

934. In regards to *"faith and works"*, we must keep taking steps, and we must keep taking responsibility.

Even so faith, if it hath not works, is dead, being alone. Yea, a man may say, Thou hast faith, and I have works: shew me thy faith without thy works, and I will shew thee my faith by my works.

– James 2:17–18

935. Unrefined, crude behavior is never a sign of success. A person may obtain money on the outside, yet if they haven't refined the person on the inside, they remain as annoying, loud, disrespectful, and dishonorable as a *painted tin foil pan!*

Though I speak with the tongues of men and of angels, and have not charity, I am become as sounding brass, or a tinkling cymbal.

–1 Corinthians 13:1

As the fining pot for silver, and the furnace for gold; so is a man to his praise.

– Proverbs 27:21

936. A pastor, preacher, or teacher is more like a *"shoe showman"*. He or she is not really *selling* shoes. Rather, they are showing you and I the best ones to take the necessary steps to reach our destination. However, if the *"shoe fits"*, we should by all means *buy it!*

Buy the truth, and sell it not; also wisdom, and instruction, and understanding.

— Proverbs 23:23

937. How can someone who came from *somewhere*, to get somewhere, despise someone who's *coming* from somewhere, to get *somewhere*?

Then he answered and spake unto me, saying, This is the word of the Lord unto Zerubbabel, saying, Not by might, nor by power, but by my spirit, saith the Lord of hosts. Who art thou, O great mountain? before Zerubbabel thou shalt become a plain: and he shall bring forth the headstone thereof with shoutings, crying, Grace, grace unto it. Moreover the word of the Lord came unto me, saying, The hands of Zerubbabel have laid the foundation of this house; his hands shall also finish it; and thou shalt know that the Lord of hosts hath sent me unto you. For who hath despised the day of small things? for they shall rejoice, and shall see the plummet in the hand of Zerubbabel with those seven; they are the eyes of the Lord, which run to and fro through the whole earth.

— Zechariah 4:6–10

938. The natural tendency of most human beings is to resist being dominated and manipulated. The natural tendency of most human beings is to attempt to dominate and manipulate others.

Not for that we have dominion over your faith, but are helpers of your joy: for by faith ye stand.

−2 Corinthians 1:24

939. Spend time in the early part of life, preparing for the later years. Make the most of the morning, so that you will have bread in the evening. Spend time in the summer, preparing for winter. Start where you are, to prepare for where you are going.

Go to the ant, thou sluggard; consider her ways, and be wise: which having no guide, overseer, or ruler, provideth her meat in the summer, and gathereth her food in the harvest.

– Proverbs 6:6–8

So teach us to number our days, that we may apply our hearts unto wisdom.

– Psalm 90:12

There be four things which are little upon the earth, but they are exceeding wise: the ants are a people not strong, yet they prepare their meat in the summer.

– Proverbs 30:24–25

In the morning sow thy seed, and in the evening withhold not thine hand: for thou knowest not whether shall prosper, either this or that, or whether they both shall be alike good.

– Ecclesiastes 11:6

940. Do not accept the peril of the times, without choosing to make a difference. The times do not determine the

outcome of the future: *people do*. And you and I are the ones to choose.

This know also, that in the last days perilous times shall come. For men shall be lovers of their own selves, covetous, boasters, proud, blasphemers, disobedient to parents, unthankful, unholy, Without natural affection, trucebreakers, false accusers, incontinent, fierce, despisers of those that are good, Traitors, heady, highminded, lovers of pleasures more than lovers of God; Having a form of godliness, but denying the power thereof: from such turn away.

–2 Timothy 3:1–5

Run ye to and fro through the streets of Jerusalem, and see now, and know, and seek in the broad places thereof, if ye can find a man, if there be any that executeth judgment, that seeketh the truth; and I will pardon it.

– Jeremiah 5:1

941. Don't make any excuses. Just do what you need to do. It will get easier, as you actually begin to *do it*.

For a dream cometh through the multitude of business; and a fool's voice is known by multitude of words.

– Ecclesiastes 5:3

942. People often seek to disregard or discredit, what they are not. Artists are often viewed as strange, until they complete the *Sistine chapel*. Musicians are often considered

odd, until they complete the *Hallelujah Chorus*. Inventors are often considered quacks, until they invent the *light bulb!*

Then he answered and spake unto me, saying, This is the word of the Lord unto Zerubbabel, saying, Not by might, nor by power, but by my spirit, saith the Lord of hosts. Who art thou, O great mountain? before Zerubbabel thou shalt become a plain: and he shall bring forth the headstone thereof with shoutings, crying, Grace, grace unto it. Moreover the word of the Lord came unto me, saying, The hands of Zerubbabel have laid the foundation of this house; his hands shall also finish it; and thou shalt know that the Lord of hosts hath sent me unto you. For who hath despised the day of small things? for they shall rejoice, and shall see the plummet in the hand of Zerubbabel with those seven; they are the eyes of the Lord, which run to and fro through the whole earth.

– Zechariah 4:6–10

943. Stop complaining, and just *get busy!*

For a dream cometh through the multitude of business; and a fool's voice is known by multitude of words.

– Ecclesiastes 5:3

944. The greatest gift and responsibility that you and I have to give to our families and others, is to succeed. That's the only way we can do our *part*. If you don't succeed, you fail to do your part! And you can't help anyone else.

As every man hath received the gift, even so minister the same one to another, as good stewards of the manifold grace of God.

−1 Peter 4:10

945. There's no rest for a poor man! He's got to get back to work, working on the right things, to save himself and his family! He can rest when he makes some *money!*

A good man leaveth an inheritance to his children's children and the wealth of the sinner is laid up for the just.

− Proverbs 13:22

He that tilleth his land shall be satisfied with bread: but he that followeth vain persons is void of understanding.

− Proverbs 12:11

So teach us to number our days, that we may apply our hearts unto wisdom.

− Psalm 90:12

Much food is in the tillage of the poor: but there is that is destroyed for want of judgment.

− Proverbs 13:23

He that walketh with wise men shall be wise: but a companion of fools shall be destroyed.

— Proverbs 13:20

946. Mistakes give you information. Learning gives you wisdom. Discernment and submission determines if you will be wise.

Hear counsel, and receive instruction, that thou mayest be wise in thy latter end.

— Proverbs 19:20

947. Miracles happen *sometimes*. Principles happen all the time. Believe for miracles, but invest in principles.

And that ye study to be quiet, and to do your own business, and to work with your own hands, as we commanded you; that ye may walk honestly toward them that are without, and that ye may have lack of nothing.

—1 Thessalonians 4:11–12

948. God's blessing of prosperity and success is *inclusive* of every person. It is not exclusive of any person. We simply must look at what God's Word has promised, look at the examples in the Bible and in today's world, and say, "*Me too!*" Then go for it!

Every man also to whom God hath given riches and wealth, and hath given him power to eat thereof, and to take his portion, and to rejoice in his labour; this is the gift of God.

– Ecclesiastes 5:19

949. What once seemed impossible becomes easier, once you actually start doing it!

Whatsoever thy hand findeth to do, do it with thy might; for there is no work, nor device, nor knowledge, nor wisdom, in the grave, whither thou goest.

– Ecclesiastes 9:10

950. Love is truly all we need, because true love inspires other actions. The just shall live by faith. However, faith works by love. We should do all things regarding life, such as working, business, giving, etc.; through the inspiration of *unfeigned love!*

For in Jesus Christ neither circumcision availeth any thing, nor uncircumcision; but faith which worketh by love.

– Galatians 5:6

951. Start the morning on your knees, in God's Word and prayer, so that you can spend the remainder of the day *standing strong!*

Finally, my brethren, be strong in the Lord, and in the power of his might. Put on the whole armour of God, that ye may be able to stand against the wiles of the devil. For we wrestle not against flesh and blood, but against principalities, against powers, against the rulers of the darkness of this world,

against spiritual wickedness in high places. Wherefore take unto you the whole armour of God, that ye may be able to withstand in the evil day, and having done all, to stand. Stand therefore, having your loins girt about with truth, and having on the breastplate of righteousness; And your feet shod with the preparation of the gospel of peace; Above all, taking the shield of faith, wherewith ye shall be able to quench all the fiery darts of the wicked. And take the helmet of salvation, and the sword of the Spirit, which is the word of God: Praying always with all prayer and supplication in the Spirit, and watching thereunto with all perseverance and supplication for all saints.

– Ephesians 6:10–18

952. When faced with unfair behavior from others, do not fret, because God is a righteous and all–seeing *judge*. He will reward every person according to their works; and He will defend you. God is our refuge and strength, a very present help in trouble.

Truly my soul waiteth upon God: from him cometh my salvation. He only is my rock and my salvation; he is my defence; I shall not be greatly moved. How long will ye imagine mischief against a man? ye shall be slain all of you: as a bowing wall shall ye be, and as a tottering fence. They only consult to cast him down from his excellency: they delight in lies: they bless with their mouth, but they curse inwardly. Selah. My soul, wait thou only upon God; for my expectation is from him. He only is my rock and my salvation: he is my defence; I shall not be moved. In God is my salvation and my

glory: the rock of my strength, and my refuge, is in God. Trust in him at all times; ye people, pour out your heart before him: God is a refuge for us. Selah. Surely men of low degree are vanity, and men of high degree are a lie: to be laid in the balance, they are altogether lighter than vanity. Trust not in oppression, and become not vain in robbery: if riches increase, set not your heart upon them. God hath spoken once; twice have I heard this; that power belongeth unto God. Also unto thee, O Lord, belongeth mercy: for thou renderest to every man according to his work.

– Psalm 62

953. Continue to take on challenging deeds, for as you continue in them, you will gain strength to do what once seemed almost *impossible!*

The righteous also shall hold on his way, and he that hath clean hands shall be stronger and stronger.

– Job 17:9

Whatsoever thy hand findeth to do, do it with thy might; for there is no work, nor device, nor knowledge, nor wisdom, in the grave, whither thou goest.

– Ecclesiastes 9:10

I can do all things through Christ, which strengtheneth me.

– Philippians 4:13

For with God nothing shall be impossible.

– Luke 1:37

954. Think success! Speak success! Act success! And you will *be* a success!

This book of the law shall not depart out of thy mouth; but thou shalt meditate therein day and night, that thou mayest observe to do according to all that is written therein: for then thou shalt make thy way prosperous, and then thou shalt have good success.

– Joshua 1:8

955. If you keep working hard, and working smart, you will eventually *"work up"* on something that will *enrich* your life forever!

And let us not be weary in well doing: for in due season we shall reap, if we faint not.

– Galatians 6:9

956. Thank God for *"haters!"* They increase your reasons and tenacity, to fight with a vengeance for success! And at the end of the day, the freehearted person will have nothing left but rejoicing, because it was never about your haters anyway!

And in nothing terrified by your adversaries: which is to them an evident token of perdition, but to you of salvation, and that of God.

– Philippians 1:28

957. Never fail to measure the treasure inside of you. No matter how much added value others bring to your life, whether through school, relationships, or business alliances, always remember that *"Rumpelstiltskin"* will always seek something of higher value, in exchange for spinning your perceived *"straw"* into *gold!*

It is naught, it is naught, saith the buyer: but when he is gone his way, then he boasteth.

– Proverbs 20:14

958. Never underestimate an opportunity. Look at opportunities, as opportunities that make other opportunities. An opportunity is a seed, containing a tree of other opportunities; each containing seeds for an *orchard* of lifetime provision!

Hope deferred maketh the heart sick: but *when* the desire cometh, *it is* a tree of life.

– Proverbs 13:12

959. We may underestimate our own ability; but never underestimate the power of God's Word. The Word is a *"seed"*. It can break through *concrete!*

Now the parable is this: The seed is the word of God. Those by the way side are they that hear; then cometh the devil, and

taketh away the word out of their hearts, lest they should believe and be saved. They on the rock are they, which, when they hear, receive the word with joy; and these have no root, which for a while believe, and in time of temptation fall away. And that which fell among thorns are they, which, when they have heard, go forth, and are choked with cares and riches and pleasures of this life, and bring no fruit to perfection. But that on the good ground are they, which in an honest and good heart, having heard the word, keep it, and bring forth fruit with patience.

– Luke 8:11–15

The prophet that hath a dream, let him tell a dream; and he that hath my word, let him speak my word faithfully. What is the chaff to the wheat? saith the Lord. Is not my word like as a fire? saith the Lord; and like a hammer that breaketh the rock in pieces?

– Jeremiah 23:28–29

960. When you get desperate enough for change, you will develop an *appetite* for wisdom!

When wisdom entereth into thine heart, and knowledge is pleasant unto thy soul; Discretion shall preserve thee, understanding shall keep thee.

– Proverbs 2:10–11

961. A nation of abominations, will suffer the divine judgment of God. A nation led by those that pervert truth, will go astray. Only through obeying God's natural, moral, and spiritual laws, will our nation be blessed! May God have mercy on the United States of America. In Jesus name. Amen.

If the foundations be destroyed, what can the righteous do?

– Psalm 11:3

The wicked shall be turned into hell, and all the nations that forget God.

– Psalm 9:17

When the righteous are in authority, the people rejoice: but when the wicked beareth rule, the people mourn.

– Proverbs 29:2

962. We should continue to go to church, even when we have *"a lot of stuff to do"*. Because, if you stop honoring God, you may run out of stuff to do, like becoming *unemployed!* Honor the God that gave you *"stuff to do!"*

Not forsaking the assembling of ourselves together, as the manner of some is; but exhorting one another: and so much the more, as ye see the day approaching.

– Hebrews 10:25

963. Only through *acting* on the Word, do we give the Word an opportunity to work in our lives. Miracles do happen to those who act on the Word of God!

Even so faith, if it hath not works, is dead, being alone. Yea, a man may say, Thou hast faith, and I have works: shew me thy faith without thy works, and I will shew thee my faith by my works.

– James 2:17–18

964. Practice makes *prepared.*

Prepare thy work without, and make it fit for thyself in the field; and afterwards build thine house.

– Proverbs 24:27

965. You must be able to hear and observe information and data, and then discern what is *relevant*, and what to ignore. If it doesn't build your faith to achieve your purpose, do not be moved.

While he yet spake, there came from the ruler of the synagogue's house certain which said, Thy daughter is dead: why troublest thou the Master any further? As soon as Jesus heard the word that was spoken, he saith unto the ruler of the synagogue, Be not afraid, only believe.

– Mark 5:35–36

966. God wants you to succeed, even more than you want to succeed. So, when you do your required part, success is guaranteed!

Every man also to whom God hath given riches and wealth, and hath given him power to eat thereof, and to take his portion, and to rejoice in his labour; this is the gift of God.

– Ecclesiastes 5:19

967. The key to your success is not a college education. It's not a high paying job. It's not finding favor with another person. No! The key to your success is becoming *"focused"* on a particular gift, talent, or inclination that contains value to others, and practicing, preparing, and becoming skillful enough that people will pay you for it, and then *sticking with it!*

Seest thou a man diligent in his business? he shall stand before kings; he shall not stand before mean men.

– Proverbs 22:29

968. Praise and worship is *"medicine"* that has no side effects, yet it has great *effects!* It will save your soul (mind, will, and emotions) and deliver your body and family. It will help you on your job and in school. Praise and worship has great effects and no side effects!

A merry heart doeth good like a medicine: but a broken spirit drieth the bones.

— Proverbs 17:22

All the days of the afflicted are evil: but he that is of a merry heart hath a continual feast.

— Proverbs 15:15

Make a joyful noise unto the Lord, all ye lands. Serve the Lord with gladness: come before his presence with singing. Know ye that the Lord he is God: it is he that hath made us, and not we ourselves; we are his people, and the sheep of his pasture. Enter into his gates with thanksgiving, and into his courts with praise: be thankful unto him, and bless his name. For the Lord is good; his mercy is everlasting; and his truth endureth to all generations.

— Psalm 100

969. Whether by miracle, or by *method*, if you continue to do the right thing, you will be successful.

Now there cried a certain woman of the wives of the sons of the prophets unto Elisha, saying, Thy servant my husband is dead; and thou knowest that thy servant did fear the Lord: and the creditor is come to take unto him my two sons to be bondmen. And Elisha said unto her, What shall I do for thee? tell me, what hast thou in the house? And she said, Thine handmaid hath not any thing in the house, save a pot of oil. Then he said, Go, borrow thee vessels abroad of all thy neighbours, even empty vessels; borrow not a few. And when thou art come in, thou shalt shut the door upon thee and upon thy sons, and shalt pour out into all those vessels, and thou

shalt set aside that which is full. So she went from him, and shut the door upon her and upon her sons, who brought the vessels to her; and she poured out. And it came to pass, when the vessels were full, that she said unto her son, Bring me yet a vessel. And he said unto her, There is not a vessel more. And the oil stayed. Then she came and told the man of God. And he said, Go, sell the oil, and pay thy debt, and live thou and thy children of the rest.

–2 Kings 4:1–7

970. Don't be afraid to give sacrificially, because often the cost of the sacrifice is less than the value of the reward.

There is that scattereth, and yet increaseth; and there is that withholdeth more than is meet, but it tendeth to poverty. The liberal soul shall be made fat: and he that watereth shall be watered also himself.

– Proverbs 11:24–25

971. Certain actions on a national, state, or local level, will bring confusion and erosion of the financial, moral, and social fiber of the fabric of society. In spite of the agendas of agreeing parties, the consequences will be forthcoming, and irrepressible, but by prayer and moral *repentance.*

Every one that is proud in heart is an abomination to the Lord: though hand join in hand, he shall not be unpunished.

– Proverbs 16:5

972. If you're waiting for everything to be perfect, before you will be happy, all I can say is *"see you at the top!"* Only in heaven will everything in our lives be perfect. In the meantime, we have to *rejoice by choice!*

And God shall wipe away all tears from their eyes; and there shall be no more death, neither sorrow, nor crying, neither shall there be any more pain: for the former things are passed away. And he that sat upon the throne said, Behold, I make all things new. And he said unto me, Write: for these words are true and faithful. And he said unto me, It is done. I am Alpha and Omega, the beginning and the end. I will give unto him that is athirst of the fountain of the water of life freely. He that overcometh shall inherit all things; and I will be his God, and he shall be my son. But the fearful, and unbelieving, and the abominable, and murderers, and whoremongers, and sorcerers, and idolaters, and all liars, shall have their part in the lake which burneth with fire and brimstone: which is the second death.

– Revelation 21:4–8

973. Nothing is guaranteed, but failure, if you don't *try.*

But without faith it is impossible to please him: for he that cometh to God must believe that he is, and that he is a rewarder of them that diligently seek him.

– Hebrews 11:6

974. When you have given to serve the Lord, you can always expect an abundant harvest in exchange. As you freely give, he will profusely reward you. However, it takes faith to give, as well as to receive. Both require *stretching*.

And it came to pass, that, as the people pressed upon him to hear the word of God, he stood by the lake of Gennesaret, And saw two ships standing by the lake: but the fishermen were gone out of them, and were washing their nets. And he entered into one of the ships, which was Simon's, and prayed him that he would thrust out a little from the land. And he sat down, and taught the people out of the ship. Now when he had left speaking, he said unto Simon, Launch out into the deep, and let down your nets for a draught. And Simon answering said unto him, Master, we have toiled all the night, and have taken nothing: nevertheless at thy word I will let down the net. And when they had this done, they inclosed a great multitude of fishes: and their net brake. And they beckoned unto their partners, which were in the other ship, that they should come and help them. And they came, and filled both the ships, so that they began to sink. When Simon Peter saw it, he fell down at Jesus' knees, saying, Depart from me; for I am a sinful man, O Lord. For he was astonished, and all that were with him, at the draught of the fishes, which they had taken: And so was also James, and John, the sons of Zebedee, which were partners with Simon. And Jesus said unto Simon, Fear not; from henceforth thou shalt catch men. And when they had brought their ships to land, they forsook all, and followed him.

– Luke 5:1–11

975. Stations and positions of power are only temporary. We each may get an opportunity to get our chance. How we exercise our turn, will be remembered far longer, than the reality of whether we actually *merited* being on top.

God that made the world and all things therein, seeing that he is Lord of heaven and earth, dwelleth not in temples made with hands; Neither is worshipped with men's hands, as though he needed any thing, seeing he giveth to all life, and breath, and all things; And hath made of one blood all nations of men for to dwell on all the face of the earth, and hath determined the times before appointed, and the bounds of their habitation; That they should seek the Lord, if haply they might feel after him, and find him, though he be not far from every one of us: For in him we live, and move, and have our being; as certain also of your own poets have said, For we are also his offspring.

– Acts 17:24–28

976. Overcome fear with confidence, competence, excellence, and *productivity*. The more you do, the better you get, and, thus, the more competent and confident. The better you do it, the more excellent you become at it. Increase productivity, to decrease fear. Overcome evil, with *good*.

The desire accomplished is sweet to the soul: but it is abomination to fools to depart from evil.

– Proverbs 13:19

977. When you are living on purpose, and you're living on assignment, God can direct you through your spirit, faster than your mind can conceive. The just shall live by faith! Write the vision, and make it plain. Then allow the Holy Spirit to lead you to its fulfillment. It takes courage, faith, hope, and trust.

And the Lord answered me, and said, Write the vision, and make it plain upon tables, that he may run that readeth it. For the vision is yet for an appointed time, but at the end it shall speak, and not lie: though it tarry, wait for it; because it will surely come, it will not tarry. Behold, his soul which is lifted up is not upright in him: but the just shall live by his faith.

– Habakkuk 2:2–4

978. God gave *gifts* to all men, however, only a few have the diligence, drive, discipline, and determination to develop their gifts and use it profusely and prolifically. However, those that do will be well recognized and rewarded both in earth and heaven. God wishes above all things that we prosper and be in health, even as our souls prosper. May we be followers of the "*examples*" of productivity!

Wherefore he saith, When he ascended up on high, he led captivity captive, and gave gifts unto men.

– Ephesians 4:8

Seest thou a man diligent in his business? he shall stand before kings; he shall not stand before mean men.

– Proverbs 22:29

979. Don't say bad things about yourself. Say good things about yourself. People will believe, what *you* believe about yourself.

For as he thinketh in his heart, so is he...

– Proverbs 23:7a

980. Don't just do things by inspiration, do things by *preparation.*

The preparations of the heart in man, and the answer of the tongue, is from the Lord.

– Proverbs 16:1

981. There's a *method* behind greatness.

He that walketh with wise men shall be wise: but a companion of fools shall be destroyed.

– Proverbs 13:20

982. You go up, *before* you go up. The new position outwardly, is a manifestation of the new position *inwardly.*

For promotion cometh neither from the east, nor from the west, nor from the south. But God is the judge: he putteth down one, and setteth up another.

– Psalm 75:6–7

983. The habit of *continual* lateness is a sign of disrespect for time and people.

Say not ye, There are yet four months, and then cometh harvest? Behold, I say unto you, Lift up your eyes, and look on the fields; for they are white already to harvest.

–John 4:35

Boast not thyself of tomorrow; for thou knowest not what a day may bring forth.

–Proverbs 27:1

So teach us to number our days, that we may apply our hearts unto wisdom.

–Psalm 90:12

984. If you will serve with excellence *by choice*, you will never be a slave.

The hand of the diligent shall bear rule: but the slothful shall be under tribute.

– Proverbs 12:24

985. Stretches of faith allow you to go beyond normal limitations of life. Take stretches of faith, and you will go *beyond the limits!*

Then saith he to the man, Stretch forth thine hand. And he stretched it forth; and it was restored whole, like as the other.

– Matthew 12:13

Enlarge the place of thy tent, and let them stretch forth the curtains of thine habitations: spare not, lengthen thy cords, and strengthen thy stakes.

– Isaiah 54:2

986. Make a *wish!* Your "*wish*" is God's command. "*W.I.S.H*" is defined "Work. Initiates. Something. Happening". So go ahead, make a *W.I.S.H!*

For a dream cometh through the multitude of business; and a fool's voice is known by multitude of words.

– Ecclesiastes 5:3

In all labour there is profit: but the talk of the lips tendeth only to penury.

– Proverbs 14:23

987. Certain money is *"trust money"*. It requires you to trust, when you invest it, that it will bring forth a harvest. Other money is *"investment money"*. It requires wisdom and discretion to multiply it over time. Invest *trust money* by faith, and believe that God will protect it. Then invest *"sure money"* by wise judgment to ensure that it multiplies in time.

Distinguished Wisdom Presents . . . "Living Proverbs"–Vol.2

Cast thy bread upon the waters: for thou shalt find it after many days. Give a portion to seven, and also to eight; for thou knowest not what evil shall be upon the earth. If the clouds be full of rain, they empty themselves upon the earth: and if the tree fall toward the south, or toward the north, in the place where the tree falleth, there it shall be. He that observeth the wind shall not sow; and he that regardeth the clouds shall not reap. As thou knowest not what is the way of the spirit, nor how the bones do grow in the womb of her that is with child: even so thou knowest not the works of God who maketh all. In the morning sow thy seed, and in the evening withhold not thine hand: for thou knowest not whether shall prosper, either this or that, or whether they both shall be alike good.

– Ecclesiastes 11:1–6

988. Continual opposition give you the opportunity to develop *"bounce back power"* like a *"super ball"* which bounces back from opposition every time. The stronger the opposition, the greater the *bounce back!*

Are they ministers of Christ? (I speak as a fool) I am more; in labours more abundant, in stripes above measure, in prisons more frequent, in deaths oft. Of the Jews five times received I forty stripes save one. Thrice was I beaten with rods, once was I stoned, thrice I suffered shipwreck, a night and a day I have been in the deep; In journeyings often, in perils of waters, in perils of robbers, in perils by mine own countrymen, in perils by the heathen, in perils in the city, in perils in the wilderness, in perils in the sea, in perils among false brethren; In weariness and painfulness, in watchings

often, in hunger and thirst, in fastings often, in cold and nakedness. Beside those things that are without, that which cometh upon me daily, the care of all the churches. Who is weak, and I am not weak? who is offended, and I burn not? If I must needs glory, I will glory of the things which concern mine infirmities.

–2 Corinthians 11:23–30

989. When you know the *truth*, you don't have to be mad. Just live according to the truth you know, and truth will prevail, and so will you.

And in nothing terrified by your adversaries: which is to them an evident token of perdition, but to you of salvation, and that of God.

– Philippians 1:28

990. Reading activates the mind. An activated mind creates a liberated life. Those who refuse to read will remain slaves. Your ability to read and think, increases your ability to question; which will lead you to the conclusion, that something is not right about you being a slave, and others reigning over you, and you will make efforts to take dominion over your own life.

Also, that the soul be without knowledge, it is not good; and he that hasteth with his feet sinneth.

– Proverbs 19:2

And that ye study to be quiet, and to do your own business, and to work with your own hands, as we commanded you; that ye may walk honestly toward them that are without, and that ye may have lack of nothing.

−1 Thessalonians 4:11–12

Wisdom is good with an inheritance: and by it there is profit to them that see the sun. For wisdom is a defence, and money is a defence: but the excellency of knowledge is, that wisdom giveth life to them that have it.

− Ecclesiastes 7:11–12

991. Strangers in the kingdom may not have the *"spirit"* of the kingdom, unless indoctrinated by the foundations of the kingdom; and thus they may not have any respect for the *sacredness* of the principles, morals, and manners of the kingdom.

It came even to pass on the third day, that, behold, a man came out of the camp from Saul with his clothes rent, and earth upon his head: and so it was, when he came to David, that he fell to the earth, and did obeisance. And David said unto him, From whence comest thou? And he said unto him, Out of the camp of Israel am I escaped. And David said unto him, How went the matter? I pray thee, tell me. And he answered, That the people are fled from the battle, and many of the people also are fallen and dead; and Saul and Jonathan his son are dead also. And David said unto the young man that told him, How knowest thou that Saul and Jonathan his son be dead? And the young man that told him said, As I happened

Pastor Terrance Levise Turner

by chance upon mount Gilboa, behold, Saul leaned upon his spear; and, lo, the chariots and horsemen followed hard after him. And when he looked behind him, he saw me, and called unto me. And I answered, Here am I. And he said unto me, Who art thou? And I answered him, I am an Amalekite. He said unto me again, Stand, I pray thee, upon me, and slay me: for anguish is come upon me, because my life is yet whole in me. So I stood upon him, and slew him, because I was sure that he could not live after that he was fallen: and I took the crown that was upon his head, and the bracelet that was on his arm, and have brought them hither unto my lord. Then David took hold on his clothes, and rent them; and likewise all the men that were with him: And they mourned, and wept, and fasted until even, for Saul, and for Jonathan his son, and for the people of the Lord, and for the house of Israel; because they were fallen by the sword. And David said unto the young man that told him, Whence art thou? And he answered, I am the son of a stranger, an Amalekite. And David said unto him, How wast thou not afraid to stretch forth thine hand to destroy the Lord's anointed? And David called one of the young men, and said, Go near, and fall upon him. And he smote him that he died. And David said unto him, Thy blood be upon thy head; for thy mouth hath testified against thee, saying, I have slain the Lord's anointed.

—2 Samuel 1:2–16

992. There is an attempt to *"strip"* society naked of all godly principles, leaving us bare, to be molested by a sinister agenda of one world government, where anything that *"they"* say goes, and there remains no morals, laws, manners, or

inhibitions that prevent destruction. *"If the foundations be destroyed, what can the righteous do?"*

If the foundations be destroyed, what can the righteous do?

— Psalm 11:3

The wicked shall be turned into hell, and all the nations that forget God.

— Psalm 9:17

When the righteous are in authority, the people rejoice: but when the wicked beareth rule, the people mourn.

— Proverbs 29:2

993. Grow as you *go!*

For I am not ashamed of the gospel of Christ: for it is the power of God unto salvation to every one that believeth; to the Jew first, and also to the Greek. For therein is the righteousness of God revealed from faith to faith: as it is written, The just shall live by faith.

— Romans 1:16–17

But we all, with open face beholding as in a glass the glory of the Lord, are changed into the same image from glory to glory, even as by the Spirit of the Lord.

—2 Corinthians 3:18

They go from strength to strength, every one of them in Zion appeareth before God.

– Psalm 84:7

994. Preachers and television networks that only continue to promote *"don't worry, be happy"* messages, while the world and nations continue to *"go down the drain"*, are neglecting their first call, and *"first love"* for the kingdom of God, which is righteousness, peace, and joy in the Holy Ghost!

Unto the angel of the church of Ephesus write; These things saith he that holdeth the seven stars in his right hand, who walketh in the midst of the seven golden candlesticks; I know thy works, and thy labour, and thy patience, and how thou canst not bear them which are evil: and thou hast tried them which say they are apostles, and are not, and hast found them liars: And hast borne, and hast patience, and for my name's sake hast laboured, and hast not fainted. Nevertheless I have somewhat against thee, because thou hast left thy first love. Remember therefore from whence thou art fallen, and repent, and do the first works; or else I will come unto thee quickly, and will remove thy candlestick out of his place, except thou repent. But this thou hast, that thou hatest the deeds of the Nicolaitanes, which I also hate. He that hath an ear, let him hear what the Spirit saith unto the churches; To him that overcometh will I give to eat of the tree of life, which is in the midst of the paradise of God.

– Revelation 2:1–7

995. Every person is created in God's image and likeness, and is *"invited"* to participate in his bounty of wealth, riches, and abundance! It all starts with a made up mind to use the natural gifts, talents, and inclinations He has given you, and to diligently pursue the preordained life He had destined for you!

For we are his workmanship, created in Christ Jesus unto good works, which God hath before ordained that we should walk in them.

– Ephesians 2:10

996. Work done is work done, and it's always good to get something done, that needs to be *done!*

In all labour there is profit: but the talk of the lips tendeth only to penury.

– Proverbs 14:23

997. Every moment that we capture is *ours*. Every moment that escapes is *gone*.

Boast not thyself of to morrow; for thou knowest not what a day may bring forth.

– Proverbs 27:1

So teach us to number our days, that we may apply our hearts unto wisdom.

– Psalm 90:12

Redeeming the time, because the days are evil.

– Ephesians 5:16

998. Open your eyes wide with excitement and expectation, for the *"half has not been told"* of what's about to unfold! Do you believe? Are you in expectation? Well, God is about to surprise you with his miraculous hand of manifestation! The half has not been told, of what's about to *unfold!*

And when the queen of Sheba had seen all Solomon's wisdom, and the house that he had built, And the meat of his table, and the sitting of his servants, and the attendance of his ministers, and their apparel, and his cupbearers, and his ascent by which he went up unto the house of the Lord; there was no more spirit in her. And she said to the king, It was a true report that I heard in mine own land of thy acts and of thy wisdom. Howbeit I believed not the words, until I came, and mine eyes had seen it: and, behold, the half was not told me: thy wisdom and prosperity exceedeth the fame which I heard.

–1 Kings 10:4–7

999. The revealing of truth is *progressive*. As we continue to meditate God's Word, and do his principles, we become more and more aware of the freedom, liberty, victory, and power that come from walking with Him. Walking with Jesus is the only way to truly be free, and be who you and I were destined to be.

Then said Jesus to those Jews which believed on him, If ye continue in my word, then are ye my disciples indeed; And ye shall know the truth, and the truth shall make you free.

– John 8:31–32

He that walketh with wise men shall be wise: but a companion of fools shall be destroyed.

– Proverbs 13:20

1000. If you *must* know, you must *will* to learn. Separation unto study is the key to understanding. If you must know, you must *will* to learn.

Through desire a man, having separated himself, seeketh and intermeddleth with all wisdom.

– Proverbs 18:1

1001. Build your life from the eternal *material* of God's Word, through obeying it. Heaven and earth will pass away, but the truth of God will stand forever. You will stand forever too, if you build on His Word. You will build a legacy of truth, honesty, righteousness, success, and integrity. Build to *last*. Build on God's Word, the Bible.

For all flesh is as grass, and all the glory of man as the flower of grass. The grass withereth, and the flower thereof falleth away: But the word of the Lord endureth for ever. And this is the word, which by the gospel is preached unto you.

–1 Peter 1:24–25

1002. You're halfway through your day! God has grace for you to go *all the way!* Be a champion! Fight all the way through. You can't lose! Because God is with you! God is for you! And God is in you! Greater is He that is in you, than he that is in the world!

Thy shoes shall be iron and brass; and as thy days, so shall thy strength be.

– Deuteronomy 33:25

1003. God so loved you and I, that while we were yet sinners, He sent His Son to die on the cross to pay for our sin and redeem us from the separation that sin had brought between the Father and us. We were already completely loved, accepted, embraced, and adored by God, our Heavenly Father, before we ever entered the Earth. That's why Jesus died and rose again to get us back to Himself!

But God commendeth his love toward us, in that, while we were yet sinners, Christ died for us.

– Romans 5:8

1004. Sideline judges, have plenty of advice, but no *trophies.* They can advise you on how to play your game, but they've never won *their own!*

He that is despised, and hath a servant, is better than he that honoureth himself, and lacketh bread.

– Proverbs 12:9

1005. There will always be something to complain about, if you *choose* to. But you don't have to let it stop you from progressing. Problems are only really problems, if you let them *stop* you from advancing, because it takes faith to advance; and only by faith can we *please God*.

But without faith it is impossible to please him: for he that cometh to God must believe that he is, and that he is a rewarder of them that diligently seek him.

– Hebrews 11:6

1006. This is a *"whosoever will"* time period in the kingdom. Whosoever will let him or her *fly!* Mount up with wings like eagles! This is your time to soar! Step out in faith! God will meet you there. Whosoever will let them *fly!*

Hast thou not known? hast thou not heard, that the everlasting God, the Lord, the Creator of the ends of the earth, fainteth not, neither is weary? there is no searching of his understanding. He giveth power to the faint; and to them that have no might he increaseth strength. Even the youths shall faint and be weary, and the young men shall utterly fall: But they that wait upon the Lord shall renew their strength; they shall mount up with wings as eagles; they shall run, and not be weary; and they shall walk, and not faint.

– Isaiah 40:28–31

1007. When you make a habit of blessing people *"left and right"*, God will make a habit of blessing you *"hand over fists"*.

There is that scattereth, and yet increaseth; and there is that withholdeth more than is meet, but it tendeth to poverty. The liberal soul shall be made fat: and he that watereth shall be watered also himself.

– Proverbs 11:24–25

1008. If it were not for the dreamers there would be no *future* worth believing for.

For a dream cometh through the multitude of business; and a fool's voice is known by multitude of words.

– Ecclesiastes 5:3

1009. Live your life always *"snacking"*. Take continual times of snacking on the Word and inspirational nuggets to encourage you continually. Snippets of *nutrition* can keep you emotionally inspired to continue to do want you need to do during the day.

And Jesus answered him, saying, It is written, That man shall not live by bread alone, but by every word of God.

– Luke 4:4

1010. Life is a school, with multiple courses, and multiple *graduations.*

Give instruction to a wise man, and he will be yet wiser: teach a just man, and he will increase in learning.

– Proverbs 9:9

1011. If I'm dreaming, please don't wake me until I'm done, because *I'm working in my sleep!*

For a dream cometh through the multitude of business; and a fool's voice is known by multitude of words.

– Ecclesiastes 5:3

In the morning sow thy seed, and in the evening withhold not thine hand: for thou knowest not whether shall prosper, either this or that, or whether they both shall be alike good.

– Ecclesiastes 11:6

1012. The world seeks to put you through a *strainer*, and examine your every crevice, interest, intent, and thought under a microscope, with the intention of exposing your heart and life. God, however, honors your individuality. He allows you to pray to Him, revealing your heart, though He made and truly knows each one of us.

Search me, O God, and know my heart: try me, and know my thoughts: And see if there be any wicked way in me, and lead me in the way everlasting.

– Psalm 139:23–24

1013. Many seem to think that we don't have to *obey* God's commandments to receive His blessings, just because we are saved, and we are made righteous by the blood of Jesus, and we have grace. However, the Old and New Testaments, only promises the blessing to those who obey God's commandments.

And it shall come to pass, if thou shalt hearken diligently unto the voice of the Lord thy God, to observe and to do all his commandments which I command thee this day, that the Lord thy God will set thee on high above all nations of the earth: And all these blessings shall come on thee, and overtake thee, if thou shalt hearken unto the voice of the Lord thy God. Blessed shalt thou be in the city, and blessed shalt thou be in the field. Blessed shall be the fruit of thy body, and the fruit of thy ground, and the fruit of thy cattle, the increase of thy kine, and the flocks of thy sheep. Blessed shall be thy basket and thy store. Blessed shalt thou be when thou comest in, and blessed shalt thou be when thou goest out. The Lord shall cause thine enemies that rise up against thee to be smitten before thy face: they shall come out against thee one way, and flee before thee seven ways. The Lord shall command the blessing upon thee in thy storehouses, and in all that thou settest thine hand unto; and he shall bless thee in the land which the Lord thy God giveth thee. The Lord shall establish thee an holy people unto himself, as he hath sworn unto thee, if thou shalt keep the commandments of the Lord thy God, and walk in his ways. And all people of the earth shall see that thou art called by the name of the Lord; and they shall be

afraid of thee. And the Lord shall make thee plenteous in goods, in the fruit of thy body, and in the fruit of thy cattle, and in the fruit of thy ground, in the land which the Lord sware unto thy fathers to give thee. The Lord shall open unto thee his good treasure, the heaven to give the rain unto thy land in his season, and to bless all the work of thine hand: and thou shalt lend unto many nations, and thou shalt not borrow. And the Lord shall make thee the head, and not the tail; and thou shalt be above only, and thou shalt not be beneath; if that thou hearken unto the commandments of the Lord thy God, which I command thee this day, to observe and to do them: And thou shalt not go aside from any of the words which I command thee this day, to the right hand, or to the left, to go after other gods to serve them.

– Deuteronomy 28:1–14

1014. One of the greatest gifts we receive from a good mother is that she believes in you and accepts you, before and in spite of your success or failure. A good mother is usually your first and greatest *cheerleader*. And, if you're fortunate, you will find your own *lifelong* ally, partner, and support for the rest of life's celebrations, in your spouse.

As one whom his mother comforteth, so will I comfort you; and ye shall be comforted in Jerusalem.

– Isaiah 66:13

Whoso findeth a wife findeth a good thing, and obtaineth favour of the Lord.

— Proverbs 18:22

1015. The more you do, the more you realize you *can do*. If you want to build up your confidence to do, just *get to doing!* The more you do, the more you realize you can do!

Whatsoever thy hand findeth to do, do it with thy might; for there is no work, nor device, nor knowledge, nor wisdom, in the grave, whither thou goest.

— Ecclesiastes 9:10

I can do all things through Christ, which strengtheneth me.

— Philippians 4:13

For with God nothing shall be impossible.

— Luke 1:37

1016. When God has an abundant harvest to fill an abundant need in your life, He gives you an opportunity to sow an abundant seed. If you sow the seed on time, you will receive the harvest *in time*.

There is that scattereth, and yet increaseth; and there is that withholdeth more than is meet, but it tendeth to poverty. The liberal soul shall be made fat: and he that watereth shall be watered also himself.

— Proverbs 11:24–25

1017. Clear the *field!* Go ahead and clear the field! Stop competing with everyone and compete only with yourself. Be the best God made you to be, and if you look back, and you're still not the best, and others are better: that just means you've just got to get better! Because you haven't met your best state yet! Be the best! *Clear the field!*

But let every man prove his own work, and then shall he have rejoicing in himself alone, and not in another.

– Galatians 6:4

1018. If it seems your life is moving in "biblical years", then God is working on a "biblical blessing!" Moses was in Egypt 40 years, in the desert 40 years, before he led the Children of Israel out of Egypt to deliverance. Noah was building the Ark *100* years, and preserved humanity. Abraham was *100* years old when his first son Isaac was born. He became the *"father of faith"* and the *"father of many nations"*. God gave us the Blessing of Abraham! Biblical years, can lead to biblical blessings! It requires faith!

Now faith is the substance of things hoped for, the evidence of things not seen. For by it the elders obtained a good report. Through faith we understand that the worlds were framed by the word of God, so that things, which are seen, were not made of things, which do appear. By faith Abel offered unto God a more excellent sacrifice than Cain, by which he obtained witness that he was righteous, God testifying of his gifts: and by it he being dead yet speaketh. By faith Enoch was translated that he should not see death; and was not found,

because God had translated him: for before his translation he had this testimony, that he pleased God. But without faith it is impossible to please him: for he that cometh to God must believe that he is, and that he is a rewarder of them that diligently seek him. By faith Noah, being warned of God of things not seen as yet, moved with fear, prepared an ark to the saving of his house; by the which he condemned the world, and became heir of the righteousness, which is by faith. By faith Abraham, when he was called to go out into a place, which he should after receive for an inheritance, obeyed; and he went out, not knowing whither he went. By faith he sojourned in the land of promise, as in a strange country, dwelling in tabernacles with Isaac and Jacob, the heirs with him of the same promise: For he looked for a city which hath foundations, whose builder and maker is God. Through faith also Sara herself received strength to conceive seed, and was delivered of a child when she was past age, because she judged him faithful who had promised. Therefore sprang there even of one, and him as good as dead, so many as the stars of the sky in multitude, and as the sand which is by the sea shore innumerable. These all died in faith, not having received the promises, but having seen them afar off, and were persuaded of them, and embraced them, and confessed that they were strangers and pilgrims on the earth. For they that say such things declare plainly that they seek a country. And truly, if they had been mindful of that country from whence they came out, they might have had opportunity to have returned. But now they desire a better country, that is, an heavenly: wherefore God is not ashamed to be called their God: for he hath prepared for them a city. By faith Abraham, when he was tried, offered up Isaac: and he that had received the promises

offered up his only begotten son, Of whom it was said, That in Isaac shall thy seed be called: Accounting that God was able to raise him up, even from the dead; from whence also he received him in a figure. By faith Isaac blessed Jacob and Esau concerning things to come. By faith Jacob, when he was a dying, blessed both the sons of Joseph; and worshipped, leaning upon the top of his staff. By faith Joseph, when he died, made mention of the departing of the children of Israel; and gave commandment concerning his bones. By faith Moses, when he was born, was hid three months of his parents, because they saw he was a proper child; and they were not afraid of the king's commandment. By faith Moses, when he was come to years, refused to be called the son of Pharaoh's daughter; Choosing rather to suffer affliction with the people of God, than to enjoy the pleasures of sin for a season; Esteeming the reproach of Christ greater riches than the treasures in Egypt: for he had respect unto the recompence of the reward. By faith he forsook Egypt, not fearing the wrath of the king: for he endured, as seeing him who is invisible. Through faith he kept the passover, and the sprinkling of blood, lest he that destroyed the firstborn should touch them. By faith they passed through the Red sea as by dry land: which the Egyptians assaying to do were drowned. By faith the walls of Jericho fell down, after they were compassed about seven days. By faith the harlot Rahab perished not with them that believed not, when she had received the spies with peace. And what shall I more say? for the time would fail me to tell of Gedeon, and of Barak, and of Samson, and of Jephthae; of David also, and Samuel, and of the prophets: Who through faith subdued kingdoms, wrought righteousness, obtained promises, stopped the mouths of

lions. Quenched the violence of fire, escaped the edge of the sword, out of weakness were made strong, waxed valiant in fight, turned to flight the armies of the aliens. Women received their dead raised to life again: and others were tortured, not accepting deliverance; that they might obtain a better resurrection: And others had trial of cruel mockings and scourgings, yea, moreover of bonds and imprisonment: They were stoned, they were sawn asunder, were tempted, were slain with the sword: they wandered about in sheepskins and goatskins; being destitute, afflicted, tormented; (Of whom the world was not worthy:) they wandered in deserts, and in mountains, and in dens and caves of the earth. And these all, having obtained a good report through faith, received not the promise: God having provided some better thing for us, that they without us should not be made perfect.

– Hebrews 11

1019. In regards to how we handle life's situations, some things are problems, and some things are *personality*. Personality often makes the difference, as to whether a situation is a *real* problem or not. Improvements in thinking, improves personality, and how we handle problems.

Brethren, be not children in understanding: howbeit in malice be ye children, but in understanding be men.

–1 Corinthians 14:20

For as he thinketh in his heart, so is he...

– Proverbs 23:7a

1020. Live your life like a *water pot*, watering flowers along the way. Everywhere you go, enhance, increase, and bless the lives that you touch, and refresh those that you come in contact with. Live your life like a water pot, *watering flowers* along the way.

There is that scattereth, and yet increaseth; and there is that withholdeth more than is meet, but it tendeth to poverty. The liberal soul shall be made fat: and he that watereth shall be watered also himself.

– Proverbs 11:24–25

1021. Spend your life daily: living, giving, growing, enhancing, increasing, accumulating value, so that at the end of the day, you will have a *treasure chest* from which to draw for all eternity!

But rather seek ye the kingdom of God; and all these things shall be added unto you. Fear not, little flock; for it is your Father's good pleasure to give you the kingdom. Sell that ye have, and give alms; provide yourselves bags which wax not old, a treasure in the heavens that faileth not, where no thief approacheth, neither moth corrupteth. For where your treasure is, there will your heart be also.

– Luke 12:31–34

1022. Don't count *common*, what others would count miraculous; or you will lose the blessing that other people are gaining from what was meant to bless you too, because you

overlook the value of what you have. Don't count common, what others count miraculous.

Jesus answered and said unto her, If thou knewest the gift of God, and who it is that saith to thee, Give me to drink; thou wouldest have asked of him, and he would have given thee living water.

– John 4:10

1023. When you win within yourself, you could never lose to *someone else.*

But let every man prove his own work, and then shall he have rejoicing in himself alone, and not in another.

– Galatians 6:4

1024. Success speaks for itself, through *results.* Failure speaks for itself, through *idle words.*

For a dream cometh through the multitude of business; and a fool's voice is known by multitude of words.

– Ecclesiastes 5:3

1025. People often try to *locate you*, and put you in a category, based on their own *limited* historical references. However, they could never be totally certain, due to each of our unique destinies, and the force of individual choice. We all must live day by day, guided by prayer and God's unerring

Word. Only He sees all the contingencies regarding His plan for you.

O lord, thou hast searched me, and known me. Thou knowest my downsitting and mine uprising, thou understandest my thought afar off. Thou compassest my path and my lying down, and art acquainted with all my ways. For there is not a word in my tongue, but, lo, O Lord, thou knowest it altogether. Thou hast beset me behind and before, and laid thine hand upon me. Such knowledge is too wonderful for me; it is high, I cannot attain unto it. Whither shall I go from thy spirit? or whither shall I flee from thy presence? If I ascend up into heaven, thou art there: if I make my bed in hell, behold, thou art there. If I take the wings of the morning, and dwell in the uttermost parts of the sea; Even there shall thy hand lead me, and thy right hand shall hold me. If I say, Surely the darkness shall cover me; even the night shall be light about me. Yea, the darkness hideth not from thee; but the night shineth as the day: the darkness and the light are both alike to thee. For thou hast possessed my reins: thou hast covered me in my mother's womb. I will praise thee; for I am fearfully and wonderfully made: marvellous are thy works; and that my soul knoweth right well. My substance was not hid from thee, when I was made in secret, and curiously wrought in the lowest parts of the earth. Thine eyes did see my substance, yet being unperfect; and in thy book all my members were written, which in continuance were fashioned, when as yet there was none of them. How precious also are thy thoughts unto me, O God! how great is the sum of them! If I should count them, they are more in number than the sand: when I awake, I am still with thee.

– Psalm 139:1–18

1026. Life takes faith and trust: faith to go forward, and trust to be patient in the process.

That ye be not slothful, but followers of them who through faith and patience inherit the promises.

– Hebrews 6:12

1027. Take time to sit and write a *business plan* for the remaining years of your life. Include everything you truly desire; financially, spiritual development, educational enhancement, physical fitness, family and relationships, greater societal giving, and the legacy you want to leave behind. If we write the vision clearly, God will *hasten* His Word to perform it!

And the Lord answered me, and said, Write the vision, and make it plain upon tables, that he may run that readeth it. For the vision is yet for an appointed time, but at the end it shall speak, and not lie: though it tarry, wait for it; because it will surely come, it will not tarry. Behold, his soul, which is lifted up, is not upright in him: but the just shall live by *his* faith.

– Habakkuk 2:2–4

1028. Truth is a matter of *truth*, not belief. Belief requires effort. Truth rests on its own *merits*. The truth is the truth; it cannot lie. The truth is the truth; it can't be denied. Our *belief* of the truth is our choice.

But the hour cometh, and now is, when the true worshippers shall worship the Father in spirit and in truth: for the Father seeketh such to worship him. God is a Spirit: and they that worship him must worship him in spirit and in truth. The woman saith unto him, I know that Messias cometh, which is called Christ: when he is come, he will tell us all things.

– John 4:23–25

1029. Don't make *long–term* plans based on temporary circumstances. This too will pass.

For our light affliction, which is but for a moment, worketh for us a far more exceeding and eternal weight of glory.

–2 Corinthians 4:17

My brethren, count it all joy when ye fall into divers temptations; Knowing this, that the trying of your faith worketh patience. But let patience have her perfect work, that ye may be perfect and entire, wanting nothing.

– James 1:2–4

1030. There are *billions* of dollars of resources on this planet. There are billions of people. God owns all the resources, and God owns all the people. He can take care of you!

The earth is the Lord's, and the fulness thereof; the world, and they that dwell therein.

— Psalm 24:1

1031. Don't fear the future; rather *create it*. Be an active participant in life. Set policy. Influence the passage of laws. Embrace society with God's love and laws. Teach and train our children. Don't fear the future: create it!

Ye are the salt of the earth: but if the salt have lost his savour, wherewith shall it be salted? it is thenceforth good for nothing, but to be cast out, and to be trodden under foot of men. Ye are the light of the world. A city that is set on an hill cannot be hid. Neither do men light a candle, and put it under a bushel, but on a candlestick; and it giveth light unto all that are in the house. Let your light so shine before men, that they may see your good works, and glorify your Father, which is in heaven.

— Matthew 5:13–16

1032. The only way to get a physical manifestation of God's Kingdom in the earth is through a *spiritual* manifestation of God's Kingdom in our lives. We must be filled with God's Spirit, and manifest the *fruit of the spirit* on our jobs, in school, in our neighborhoods, in our families, and with strangers. The greater the spiritual manifestation will result in the greater physical manifestation.

When they therefore were come together, they asked of him, saying, Lord, wilt thou at this time restore again the kingdom to Israel? And he said unto them, It is not for you to know the times or the seasons, which the Father hath put in his own

power. But ye shall receive power, after that the Holy Ghost is come upon you: and ye shall be witnesses unto me both in Jerusalem, and in all Judaea, and in Samaria, and unto the uttermost part of the earth.

– Acts 1:6–8

And when he was demanded of the Pharisees, when the kingdom of God should come, he answered them and said, The kingdom of God cometh not with observation: Neither shall they say, Lo here! or, lo there! for, behold, the kingdom of God is within you.

– Luke 17:20–21

But seek ye first the kingdom of God, and his righteousness; and all these things shall be added unto you.

– Matthew 6:33

For the kingdom of God is not meat and drink; but righteousness, and peace, and joy in the Holy Ghost.

– Romans 14:17

But the fruit of the Spirit is love, joy, peace, longsuffering, gentleness, goodness, faith, Meekness, temperance: against such there is no law.

– Galatians 5:22–23

1033. Live your life with your feet firmly rooted stably on the ground. Have the ability to envision *Heavens' realities*, and

have and use the faith and skill necessary to bring those realities into the earth, through practical decision-making and actions.

So teach us to number our days, that we may apply our hearts unto wisdom.

— Psalm 90:12

1034. Go ahead and *step out* and trust God. It is worth it! He will prove Himself faithful to those that trust Him. His promises are true. His principles are trustworthy. His lifetime rewards are abundant!

O taste and see that the Lord is good: blessed is the man that trusteth in him. O fear the Lord, ye his saints: for there is no want to them that fear him. The young lions do lack, and suffer hunger: but they that seek the Lord shall not want any good thing.

— Psalm 34:8–10

1035. God's nature is to willingly give you a multitude of things *without* you earning it: like mercy, grace, favor, forgiveness, a chance, etc. However, mankind's nature is to give you an abundance of things, *only* when you earn it. *Both* are influenced by God's nature relating to the Earth.

Give, and it shall be given unto you; good measure, pressed down, and shaken together, and running over, shall men give

into your bosom. For with the same measure that ye mete withal it shall be measured to you again.

– Luke 6:38

1036. If you are diligent, you don't need an abusive *taskmaster*. You are qualified to work for yourself, if you so desire. Work as unto the Lord: He's not abusive, and He's not unfair.

Go to the ant, thou sluggard; consider her ways, and be wise: which having no guide, overseer, or ruler, provideth her meat in the summer, and gathereth her food in the harvest.

– Proverbs 6:6–8

And whatsoever ye do, do it heartily, as to the Lord, and not unto men; knowing that of the Lord ye shall receive the reward of the inheritance: for ye serve the Lord Christ.

– Colossians 3:23–24

Seest thou a man diligent in his business? he shall stand before kings; he shall not stand before mean men.

– Proverbs 22:29

1037. No matter how close or how far you are from your goals, the fact that you have goals and are steadily working towards your goals, means you are a success! You're closer today than you have ever been before. You are a success!

Now therefore perform the doing of it; that as there was a readiness to will, so there may be a performance also out of that which ye have. For if there be first a willing mind, it is accepted according to that a man hath, and not according to that he hath not.

–2 Corinthians 8:11–12

1038. A word of wisdom to husbands and wives: *regular* sexual fulfillment within the marriage reduces the risk of being influenced by *outside* temptations.

The wife hath not power of her own body, but the husband: and likewise also the husband hath not power of his own body, but the wife. Defraud ye not one the other, except it be with consent for a time, that ye may give yourselves to fasting and prayer; and come together again, that Satan tempt you not for your incontinency.

–1 Corinthians 7:4–5

Nevertheless, to avoid fornication, let every man have his own wife, and let every woman have her own husband.

–1 Corinthians 7:2

1039. As we live day to day, taking care of the demands of life, and striving for all the things we want, let us all live in such a way, that we will be counted worthy to *"be in that number, when the saints go marching in!"* Jesus is coming soon!

But, beloved, be not ignorant of this one thing, that one day *is* with the Lord as a thousand years, and a thousand years as one day. The Lord is not slack concerning his promise, as some men count slackness; but is longsuffering to us–ward, not willing that any should perish, but that all should come to repentance. But the day of the Lord will come as a thief in the night; in the which the heavens shall pass away with a great noise, and the elements shall melt with fervent heat, the earth also and the works that are therein shall be burned up.

–2 Peter 3:8–10

For this we say unto you by the word of the Lord, that we, which are alive and remain unto the coming of the Lord shall not prevent them, which are asleep. For the Lord himself shall descend from heaven with a shout, with the voice of the archangel, and with the trump of God: and the dead in Christ shall rise first: Then we which are alive and remain shall be caught up together with them in the clouds, to meet the Lord in the air: and so shall we ever be with the Lord.

–1 Thessalonians 4:15–17

1040. Anytime you try to find the truth apart from God, you get *weird!*

There is no [human] wisdom or understanding or counsel [that can prevail] against the Lord.

– Proverbs 21:30

Amplified Bible (AMP)

1041. A big dream, plus big preparation, equals big success! Dream big, and then prepare big, in order to accomplish your big dream. God needs big dreamers, willing to prepare to accomplish the dreams he put in your heart! Preparation makes the difference between dreams and reality.

For a dream cometh through the multitude of business; and a fool's voice is known by multitude of words.

– Ecclesiastes 5:3

In the morning sow thy seed, and in the evening withhold not thine hand: for thou knowest not whether shall prosper, either this or that, or whether they both shall be alike good.

– Ecclesiastes 11:6

1042. A good negotiator is like a good *parent*. You acknowledge and deal with your child's objections, but in the end you have the responsibility to make sure that the child eats the *spinach!*

It is naught, it is naught, saith the buyer: but when he is gone his way, then he boasteth.

– Proverbs 20:14

1043. *Saturday* is a great day to enjoy your family and home. It is a blessed day of rest, recreation, and restoration. It is a day to worship God, and to get new ideas for your future.

Even the Devil has to be at peace with you on Saturday. He can't curse, what God has *blessed!*

And God blessed them, and God said unto them, Be fruitful, and multiply, and replenish the earth, and subdue it: and have dominion over the fish of the sea, and over the fowl of the air, and over every living thing that moveth upon the earth.

– Genesis 1:28

Thus the heavens and the earth were finished, and all the host of them. And on the seventh day God ended his work, which he had made; and he rested on the seventh day from all his work, which he had made. And God blessed the seventh day, and sanctified it: because that in it he had rested from all his work which God created and made.

– Genesis 2:1–3

Hast not thou made an hedge about him, and about his house, and about all that he hath on every side? thou hast blessed the work of his hands, and his substance is increased in the land.

– Job 1:10

Behold, I have received commandment to bless: and he hath blessed; and I cannot reverse it.

– Numbers 23:20

1044. When you work hard, you deserve the reward.

Then he answered and spake unto me, saying, This is the word of the Lord unto Zerubbabel, saying, Not by might, nor by power, but by my spirit, saith the Lord of hosts. Who art thou, O great mountain? before Zerubbabel thou shalt become a plain: and he shall bring forth the headstone thereof with shoutings, crying, Grace, grace unto it. Moreover the word of the Lord came unto me, saying, The hands of Zerubbabel have laid the foundation of this house; his hands shall also finish it; and thou shalt know that the Lord of hosts hath sent me unto you. For who hath despised the day of small things? for they shall rejoice, and shall see the plummet in the hand of Zerubbabel with those seven; they are the eyes of the Lord, which run to and fro through the whole earth.

– Zechariah 4:6–10

1045. People with money, look for people with *vision*. Money follows vision.

And the Lord answered me, and said, Write the vision, and make it plain upon tables, that he may run that readeth it. For the vision is yet for an appointed time, but at the end it shall speak, and not lie: though it tarry, wait for it; because it will surely come, it will not tarry. Behold, his soul which is lifted up is not upright in him: but the just shall live by his faith.

– Habakkuk 2:2–4

1046. There's enough money to do just about anything that needs to be done. However, there's not enough vision, nor

enough people who are committed to bring the vision to pass. We must pray for vision, and we must pray for *laborers.*

And the child Samuel ministered unto the Lord before Eli. And the word of the Lord was precious in those days; there was no open vision.

–1 Samuel 3:1

Pray ye therefore the Lord of the harvest, that he will send forth labourers into his harvest.

– Matthew 9:38

1047. The first place of *profitability* is to believe in yourself, and what you have to offer. You will never be profitable, if you don't first of all, believe in yourself, and what you have to offer.

But let every man prove his own work, and then shall he have rejoicing in himself alone, and not in another.

– Galatians 6:4

Wherefore I perceive that there is nothing better, than that a man should rejoice in his own works; for that is his portion: for who shall bring him to see what shall be after him?

– Ecclesiastes 3:22

Every man also to whom God hath given riches and wealth, and hath given him power to eat thereof, and to take his portion, and to rejoice in his labour; this is the gift of God.

— Ecclesiastes 5:19

1048. Sometimes life moves faster than you have time to figure out. During those times, you must remember and trust that God has your life in His hands, and He's already worked it out!

The steps of a good man are ordered by the Lord: and he delighteth in his way.

— Psalm 37:23

And we know that all things work together for good to them that love God, to them who are the called according to his purpose. For whom he did foreknow, he also did predestinate to be conformed to the image of his Son, that he might be the firstborn among many brethren.

— Romans 8:28–29

1049. Every part played in the positive performance of God's perfect plan, is crucial to the end result, and survival of the world. You may never know until much later, how important you are to God's plan, when you perform God's perfect will.

For if thou altogether holdest thy peace at this time, then shall there enlargement and deliverance arise to the Jews from another place; but thou and thy father's house shall be destroyed: and who knoweth whether thou art come to the kingdom for such a time as this?

— Esther 4:14

1050. In the world in which we live, we have to know what to *accept*, and we have to know what to *fight* to change. We must allow the Bible to guide us. We must be willing to *stand up* and make a difference.

For if thou altogether holdest thy peace at this time, then shall there enlargement and deliverance arise to the Jews from another place; but thou and thy father's house shall be destroyed: and who knoweth whether thou art come to the kingdom for such a time as this?

— Esther 4:14

1051. The *principles* of Jesus will make you successful. The *person* of Jesus will make you a success. As you study His principles, you can develop success habits. As you fellowship with Him, you can develop His heart. Spend time with Jesus, in the Bible and prayer, and you will gain a relationship with Him and His wisdom.

This book of the law shall not depart out of thy mouth; but thou shalt meditate therein day and night, that thou mayest observe to do according to all that is written therein: for then thou shalt make thy way prosperous, and then thou shalt have good success.

— Joshua 1:8

But be ye doers of the word, and not hearers only, deceiving your own selves.

– James 1:22

Come unto me, all ye that labour and are heavy laden, and I will give you rest. Take my yoke upon you, and learn of me; for I am meek and lowly in heart: and ye shall find rest unto your souls. For my yoke is easy, and my burden is light.

– Matthew 11:28–30

1052. You have the capacity, and opportunity, to make a contribution to life, that is so significant, that it *resets* the "*clock of history*" in the human story! The time to act is now!

For if thou altogether holdest thy peace at this time, then shall there enlargement and deliverance arise to the Jews from another place; but thou and thy father's house shall be destroyed: and who knoweth whether thou art come to the kingdom for such a time as this?

– Esther 4:14

1053. Success is *guaranteed*, to those who do what's necessary to succeed. Study, read, and thoroughly prepare, then, act on what you've learned. Then, success is guaranteed, to those who do what's *necessary* to succeed.

And that ye study to be quiet, and to do your own business, and to work with your own hands, as we commanded you; that ye may walk honestly toward them that are without, and that ye may have lack of nothing.

–1 Thessalonians 4:11–12

That ye be not slothful, but followers of them who through faith and patience inherit the promises.

– Hebrews 6:12

1054. Life requires a long-term view, while walking by faith day by day.

For we walk by faith, not by sight.

–2 Corinthians 5:7

But without faith it is impossible to please him: for he that cometh to God must believe that he is, and that he is a rewarder of them that diligently seek him.

– Hebrews 11:6

And the Lord answered me, and said, Write the vision, and make it plain upon tables, that he may run that readeth it. For the vision is yet for an appointed time, but at the end it shall speak, and not lie: though it tarry, wait for it; because it will surely come, it will not tarry. Behold, his soul, which is lifted up, is not upright in him: but the just shall live by *his* faith.

– Habakkuk 2:2–4

1055. If God be for you, who can be against you: and if *you* be for God, you can never fail!

What shall we then say to these things? If God be for us, who can be against us?

—Romans 8:31

Then Moses stood in the gate of the camp, and said, Who is on the Lord's side? Let him come unto me. And all the sons of Levi gathered themselves together unto him.

—Exodus 32:26

1056. This is a *new* day! Old things are passed away. This is the only time that matters. What you and I do now is what will determine the outcome of tomorrow. This is your new opportunity. Simply because you are here another day, means that God has given you and I another opportunity to *get it right* for the future. Be encouraged! You've made it to today. You can impact the future!

Therefore if any man be in Christ, he is a new creature: old things are passed away; behold, all things are become new.

—2 Corinthians 5:17

It is of the Lord's mercies that we are not consumed, because his compassions fail not. They are new every morning: great is thy faithfulness.

— Lamentations 3:22–23

1057. People who are *casual* about pursuing their destiny, either are ignorant that they have a significant destiny, or they are ignorant that the accomplishment of their destiny impacts so many more people than themselves. Pursue your destiny

like the *survival of the world* depended on it! Because a certain portion of it does!

For if thou altogether holdest thy peace at this time, then shall there enlargement and deliverance arise to the Jews from another place; but thou and thy father's house shall be destroyed: and who knoweth whether thou art come to the kingdom for such a time as this?

– Esther 4:14

1058. *Stretching exercises* along the way, prepares you for the *heavy lifting* that your destiny will require of you.

If thou faint in the day of adversity, thy strength is small.

– Proverbs 24:10

1059. Do not fear the future! You were *"custom–made"* for this time in life. You can handle whatever changes or developments that are scheduled for the future of the world. Plan to live! You will *surprise* yourself with how well you do for the future! You can handle it!

For if thou altogether holdest thy peace at this time, then shall there enlargement and deliverance arise to the Jews from another place; but thou and thy father's house shall be destroyed: and who knoweth whether thou art come to the kingdom for such a time as this?

– Esther 4:14

1060. Invest in entrepreneurial ventures. You have to "*own the game*" in order to truly *win* the game!

And that ye study to be quiet, and to do your own business, and to work with your own hands, as we commanded you; that ye may walk honestly toward them that are without, and that ye may have lack of nothing.

–1 Thessalonians 4:11–12

1061. The *foolishness* of the moral decline and degradation of good sense and values, that has occurred in our society, such as increasing abortions, same–sex marriage, legalizing marijuana use, atheism, and other impending declines; are the result of the human mind's *reasoning*, without submitting to the influence of the wisdom of God's laws and judgment. The results will always lead to decay. The only answer is to return to the *Bible*.

There is no [human] wisdom or understanding or counsel [that can prevail] against the Lord.

– Proverbs 21:30

Amplified Bible (AMP)

Every one that is proud in heart is an abomination to the Lord: though hand join in hand, he shall not be unpunished.

– Proverbs 16:5

It is an abomination to kings to commit wickedness: for the throne is established by righteousness.

– Proverbs 16:12

The fool hath said in his heart, There is no God. They are corrupt, they have done abominable works, there is none that doeth good.

– Psalm 14:1

1062. God has *answers* to the questions, issues, dangers, and possibilities of our world. If we will seek Him, He will hear and answer us. God is merciful, and He is waiting and wanting to answer our every need. He is committed to our long-term wellbeing. He loves His creation. He loves His family. He loves *you!*

For God so loved the world, that he gave his only begotten Son, that whosoever believeth in him should not perish, but have everlasting life. For God sent not his Son into the world to condemn the world; but that the world through him might be saved

– John 3:16–17

Final Word

Now that you have enjoyed *Distinguished Wisdom Presents... "Living Proverbs"–Volume 2*, I encourage you to read this book daily. Use it as a reference book for continual counsel. Many readers of *"Living Proverbs"–Volume 1* indicated the words helped to deliver their mind. One reader even gave the book to a person addicted to drugs, and they were able to find wisdom for a better way of thinking. If the mind can get free, the life can get free. The words brought peace and deliverance. God's word is a healer. As you renew your mind to His Word you will be set free. Proverbs 4:7 says, "Wisdom is the principal thing; therefore get wisdom: and with all thy getting get understanding." Therefore, I recommend that you take time to read this book over again, and allow these truths to free you. Jesus said in John 8:31–32 and 36 these words:

> Then said Jesus to those Jews, which believed on him, If ye continue in my word,

then are ye my disciples indeed: And ye shall know the truth, and the truth shall make you free. If the son therefore shall make you free, you shall be free indeed.

God's Word is what makes us free. As we renew our mind to God's Word, our lives will be changed. We will enjoy the best that He desires for us. And we will be able to teach our children, grandchildren, and those that we come in contact with how to be free indeed. Therefore, as you read this book *Distinguished Wisdom Presents... "Living Proverbs"–Volume 2*, my prayer is *"May your life be enriched by the words of wisdom!"* Be sure to look for the audiobook at www.TerranceTurnerBooks.com. You will be further enriched as you hear the words of the author in an audiobook.

About The Author

Pastor Terrance Levise Turner is the senior pastor of Faith Country Holiness Church in Gallatin, TN. Pastor Turner has an MBA in Finance and Supply Chain Management, and a Bachelor's of Speech Communications and Theater/Mass Media from Tennessee State University. Pastor Turner is the

author of several books, including the *"Living Proverbs"* series, and *Your Wealth Is In Your Anointing: Discover Keys To Releasing Your Potential*. His books and audiobooks are available at www.TerranceTurnerBooks.com. Terrance is also a singer/songwriter/recording artist. He ministers the gospel in Word and song with his wife, Avis. Their music is available at www.FaithCountryProductions.com. They live in Nashville, TN. Pastor Turner continues to serve the community and Body of Christ through service, music, and teaching the Word of God.

www.ingramcontent.com/pod-product-compliance
Lightning Source LLC
Chambersburg PA
CBHW030310080526
44584CB00012B/517